Expendable for God

The righteous shall flourish like a palm tree,
He shall grow like a cedar in Lebanon.
Those who are planted in the house of the Lord
Shall flourish in the courts of our God.
Psalm 92:12–13

Expendable for God

Seventy Years in Christian Ministry

Pedro Gutiérrez

"Expendable for God" – Pedro Gutiérrez S. and Jim Smyth
Copyright © 2018 One Mission Society
An adapted translation from the Spanish version, "Historias de un Largo Ministerio" (One Mission Society – 2016)
All rights reserved. No portion of this book may be reproduced in any form without the written permission of the publisher, except in the case of brief quotations in critical articles or reviews.
All scripture quotations, unless otherwise indicated, are taken from the Holy Bible, New King James Version (NKJV)
Front cover picture: Don Pedro contemplates the beauty of the Andes in the state of Boyacá, Colombia.
Editor: Sara Leone, Camp Hill, PA
Cover design: John Miller, Carlisle, PA
Biographical narratives, photography, and overall compilation: Jim Smyth

Printed in the United States of America
Paperback ISBN: 978-1-62245-598-0
eBook ISBN: 978-1-62245-599-7
10 9 8 7 6 5 4 3 2 1
Available where books are sold
Printed in the United States of America

One Mission Society
P.O. Box A
Greenwood, Indiana 46142
317.888.3333
www.onemissionsociety.org
http://oms.media

Contents

Preface ix

Part One

    Introduction xiii

    The Call and Early Ministry 1

    New Congregations 15

    Preparation of Leaders 39

    Attending to People in Special Need 45

Part Two

    "The Modest Giant from Quindío" 57

    Tributes 77

    Endnotes 83

Rev. Pedro Gutiérrez on his 90th birthday

Preface

During his later years, pastor and missionary Pedro Gutiérrez, *Don Pedro,* as everyone called him, noted down some accounts of his experiences. His life was dedicated to evangelization and preaching. The Good News of salvation and the teachings of the Lord Jesus were constantly his principal focus.

His early reading of the Bible awakened in him an interest that never diminished throughout his life. On the contrary, over time, his love of the Scriptures and his joy in reading them so increased that he decided he needed to study at the Bible Seminary of San José, Costa Rica.

This seminary was established by the Latin America Mission[1] and had as its goal the preparation of missionaries and pastors who would evangelize and make disciples in the Latin American world. The same mission (LAM) also sponsored the Christian Clinic in San José where nurses were prepared for humanitarian work.

In the environment of evangelical revival at the seminary, young Pedro grew spiritually, and later he was chosen to pioneer the work of evangelization on the Atlantic coast of north Colombia. Upon graduation from the seminary, he married

Fanny Hogg, a Costa Rican who had a degree in obstetrics from the University of Costa Rica. Fanny was a dedicated and competent help to him in his life and ministry. During her career, she attended the births of numerous babies and helped nursing mothers at no cost to believers, wherever she and Don Pedro worked.

In this record, "Expendable for God," Don Pedro tells of his early years when he did extensive evangelization, spreading the message of the Gospel across the land on horseback or by boat along the banks of the vast Magdalena River and its tributaries. He comes across as a very practical leader, founding churches and building houses of worship and schools according to the need, wherever he went.

After many years of ministry with the Latin America Mission and during an interlude in Costa Rica, Don Pedro became acquainted with Jim Smyth, a Britisher who had arrived at the language school in San José to learn Spanish in preparation for missionary work in Colombia with the inter-American[2] churches. Later, Pedro and Fanny Gutiérrez joined the same mission, and continued to serve in Colombia for many more years. The connection with Jim Smyth from Costa Rica days led to a close working relationship between him and Don Pedro. In later years, they traveled together, evangelizing in rural areas and cities across Colombia. In Part Two of this narrative, Jim makes reference to these years of ministry and adds other details to this biographical sketch.

It is a special honor to present this personal testimony of our father. We trust God that the record of his life given here will prove helpful and that it will be profitable and of significant benefit to the reader.

Peter Luis Gutiérrez	Juan David Gutiérrez
Baltimore, Maryland, USA	Cali, Colombia

Part One

Introduction

In this account, I am not writing my biography. I only want to tell of some events that took place in my ministry, which began in January 1938 and has continued up to this time (2004). So I am not recounting all that happened in those years, just a few relevant happenings.

Over a ten-year period, the Lord blessed me with the gift of evangelism, and I had the opportunity to serve in several foreign countries, such as Panama, Costa Rica, and Nicaragua. In Colombia, God gave me the privilege of preaching in Barranquilla and Valledupar during the Evangelism in Depth campaigns, a program of the Latin America Mission. Through this ministry, many heard the Gospel in Cali and Buenaventura also. In a large Buenaventura auditorium, the bishop and several priests were present, and every night many people came forward, confessing their sins and indicating a desire to surrender their lives to the Lord. I

Don Pedro preaches in one of the campaigns sponsored by Evangelism in Depth

also had invitations to preach in the cities of Neiva, Florencia, Armenia, and Pereira, and in the state of La Guajira. I couldn't accept them all because, at that time, I was the pastor of more than 200 people in the Magangué church.

During my ministry, I organized twelve congregations. Some of these have disappeared, either because they did not have anyone to care for them after I left, or because believers, for various reasons, had to move away. Six of those twelve congregations became formally constituted churches. These have grown in number, and have each started several daughter congregations. A few of these churches are led by pastors who originated in the local leadership. Some of them have had training in Bible institutes, but others simply prepared themselves through correspondence courses and then assumed the leadership responsibility of their congregation. For all this, may our Lord Jesus Christ be forever praised.

My Gratitude

To my Savior and Lord I owe my most profound gratitude. He saved me as a boy. He called me to His holy service in my youth and made it possible for me to prepare myself for the ministry. He has guided, supported, and helped me all through these many years of service.

I am deeply grateful to my first wife, Fanny Hogg. From our earliest years together, I benefited from her faithful prayers. Fanny took charge of the congregation while I was traveling. She served not only as a community nurse, but also as a messenger of the Gospel to the lost.

I am greatly indebted to my second wife, Teresa Lizarazo. She took me by the hand in the most difficult years of my life and helped me become re-established in my ministry. Teresa assisted me competently as a teacher, as a counselor, and as one who was born to serve. In the later years of my life, when my ministry became more difficult, she found extra employment to provide for our daily needs.

I am also a grateful debtor to my sons. As children, they were never any hindrance to my ministry. They learned to submit to the direction and discipline of their mother. As adolescents, they were accepting of our meager resources and never expected things we could not afford. Now, as adults, they have honored their mother and father and are following the Lord.

Chapter 1

The Call and Early Ministry

Getting to Know the Bible

When I was five years old, my father and mother made a trip to visit both sets of my grandparents in the state of Cundinamarca.

On the way, we passed through cold Bogotá, the capital of Colombia. While walking in the streets of the city, a man approached my father and offered to sell him a book that taught about God.

My father liked to read about God. This man invited him into a narrow passageway between two buildings and pulled a big book from under his *ruana*. He read the Ten Commandments and other portions to him. He also showed him where in the book to find different readings, and then he sold it to him for 50 cents (which, today sounds very cheap, but it wasn't then). Back home my

The beauty of the Colombian Andes

father would read the Bible to us on Sundays, at Easter, and on other holidays. He only read some selections, such as the Ten Commandments, the Sermon on the Mount, the Lord's Prayer, and the stories of the Samaritan woman and Nicodemus. He did not pray, because he did not know how to pray; he explained nothing, because he did not know how; he let the Bible speak for itself. These passages were like God's voice to me, and they had such an influence on my life that, from that time on, they have always come to mind.

Several years passed without our gaining any further knowledge of the Bible than these few passages. But, one good day, he was invited to a neighboring farm to listen to the Bible being explained. He took his older sons along with him, and there we met a man who had brought Bibles to sell. The neighbors bought their own copy, and they all seemed very happy to be able to read God's Word for the first time.

The meetings there began with the singing of the hymn entitled "Jesus Is Man's Best Friend." The evangelist sang it several times, because no one in the meeting could sing or knew anything of the Gospel. He repeated the words of the hymn over and over until we learned it. I remember nothing of the explanations that the evangelist gave, but all my life since then, those words, "Jesus is man's best Friend," have remained with me. From that night on, and every day of my life since, the Lord Jesus Christ has been my best Friend. He saved me, and He commissioned me to preach the Gospel.

First Sunday Bible School

The evangelist visited our area every three months and brought more Bibles and some material that helped us better understand this wonderful book. To help meet the needs of those who were hungering to know more of the Bible, he suggested the practical idea of appointing one of them to teach the Bible to the others in his own house. We were invited to attend at ten o'clock in the morning the following Sunday. And so began what became known as the Sunday Bible School. My brother and I always arrived before ten o'clock. The owner of the house offered us cigarettes to smoke until the others arrived. This man had not yet been converted to Jesus Christ. However, about four weeks after that, he told the class: "Evangelical Christians do not smoke. So from today on, we will not smoke."

The first Sunday meetings consisted of a Bible reading and some brief explanations, and we always ended with the Lord's Prayer, partly because our teacher did not know how to pray in his own words. Despite rather elementary explanations, the people were interested in what they heard from the Bible. Some wanted the meeting to be held in their homes as well, so the Sunday Bible School was scheduled to meet consecutively in about eight different homes. This gave other believers an opportunity to tell about their Christian experience, and the movement grew significantly throughout that rural area, which was called La Elvecia. Soon, the Cumberland Presbyterian Mission in Cali sent workers to teach us hymns and to help teach the Word of God.

Conversion to Christ

I spent my childhood and part of my youth learning Bible verses, attending the meetings faithfully, and participating in various activities such as the Christmas and Easter programs and other congregational events.

At one Wednesday prayer service, the pastor explained Romans 6:23, "For the wages of sin is death, but the gift of God is eternal life in Christ Jesus our Lord." He gave us several thoughts and put a lot of emphasis on the reality of people being punished in hell if they did not accept the gift of God, which is the Person of Jesus Christ. He made no application, nor did he give an invitation to receive Jesus Christ as the gift of God because, most likely, he expected the Lord to work in our hearts.

I was very restless when I went home that night, and I knew that the Holy Spirit had spoken to me. I knelt by my bed, and I prayed, "Lord, if I die tonight, I would be punished and would go to hell." So with all my heart and with all my strength, I prayed, "Lord, forgive my sins and have mercy on me. Forgive me, Lord." At that moment, I heard the voice of God speaking so clearly and so powerfully that I remembered it all my life. The Lord said to me, "Pedro, your sins are forgiven, and from today you will serve Me."

The next day, I woke up convinced that I must dedicate my life to work for the Lord. The following Saturday, I began to serve God and all humanity. At home, I had collected many tracts that the church gave us. On Saturdays, I was always sent to the city of Armenia to buy the weekly provisions for our family. On the road, I would often meet people returning home, and so I would give them a tract, but I didn't offer them any proper explanation of it. In the city, I would watch for people who were shopping or just looking into the store windows, and I would give them something to read. If they asked me what the tract was about and what it meant, I would only say, "Read it and you'll easily understand it." Then I would continue on my way without explaining anything. I was timid about talking to people, for indeed I was a very shy boy.

My Baptism

The Lord permitted me to do my high school studies in Cali at the American School under the auspices of the Cumberland Presbyterian Mission. A missionary gave me the required preparatory classes for holy baptism. On the day of my baptism, I had a glorious experience: I felt that the Lord Jesus Christ had taken me in His arms. There and then, I had a fresh impetus to preach the sacred Gospel.

Pastor Martiniano Fajardo took me under his care as my counselor, just as Barnabas became that special counselor to Paul. Pastor Fajardo corrected my grammar and vocabulary, and he took me along to his home meetings. After several weeks of accompanying him in these gatherings, he sometimes asked me to teach the Word in the meetings. The first few times I did it I was quite fearful, but I gradually gained confidence. When he noticed that I had gained more self-confidence and aptitude for teaching, he had me lead the Sunday Bible School class for young people. I managed to do this with pleasure, even though I still knew so little about the Bible and really next to nothing about how to teach. But to me, this was serving the Lord.

Call to Active Duty

For some time I attended all the home meetings where the Word of God was taught. Sometimes they asked me to lead the Bible study, and I did so with the intention of serving the Lord. But I wasn't satisfied with this small effort; I wanted to study so I would know the Bible well and learn how to preach to the multitudes. The congregation of La Elvecia, where I was attending, invited Alfredo Cardona to be their pastor. This was a young man from Guatemala who had completed his theological studies at the Bible Institute of Costa Rica. In fact, he was one of their first graduates. Alfredo was interested in training young people for God's work. He told me about the institute, and helped me make arrangements to study there. Later, I received a letter of approval, informing me of the date my studies would begin and including some travel guidelines.

Great Difficulties in the Way

Two major obstacles came up regarding this plan. First, I could not leave the country without completing compulsory military service. I had either to serve a year in the military or pay to be exempt. The exemption fee stipulated by the government was well beyond my means. The second difficulty was the cost of travel to San José, Costa Rica. For me, it appeared that the doors were closed. My dream of going to the Bible Institute for the preparation I needed seemed impossible. But the congregation kept praying that I would be able to go there. Every day I sought the Lord, asking Him to help me prepare myself for His service.

A month passed, and then one morning my father said to me, "Here is the money to pay for your military card, and to buy your fare to San José." I was amazed at the goodness and grace of the Lord to me. This was the first miracle I had seen in my life. God proved that indeed it was His holy will for me to go to the Bible Institute, and I took this as a promise that He would be with me and would supply all my needs. In two weeks I was able to get all my things in order, and then I was ready to go to where the Lord would change my whole future in this world.

Farewell to My Mother

The day came when I had to leave my family. My father was not at home that morning. Saying goodbye to my mother was very difficult. When the moment came, I acted on impulse, hugged her, and said, "Goodbye, Mother." She cried a lot, but I left in a hurry, as if trying to escape from the greatest sorrow I had ever felt. On the way, I went into the woods, and there, hidden among the trees, I wept for about fifteen minutes. To me, it was as if my mother and my entire family had died.

Then, just as I started to walk on, a young fellow overtook me. He was a close friend of mine and a fine Christian. Noticing that I had been crying, he began to console me. He congratulated me, and commended me for being willing to serve the Lord. He told me that the path I had chosen was the most glorious of all. He promised to pray for me, and I am sure he did. He helped me carry my suitcase until I boarded the train that would take me from Armenia to Buenaventura. There I would board the boat to Costa Rica. All my life I remembered that young man. His name is gone from my memory, but his sharing with a sad traveler like me will always live within my heart.

It was several years before I returned to my parents' home, and happily, I found them all alive and well. I loved my mother as the most precious person on earth. But that morning when we parted, I truly learned what the Lord was teaching me: "He who loves father or mother more than Me is not worthy of Me" (Matthew 10:37).

Journey to the Biblical Institute in San José, Costa Rica

New and very strange for me was that trip by sea. I went aboard ship during the night in the port city of Buenaventura on the Pacific coast of Colombia. The next morning I could see only sky and water. For the first time, I worshiped the Lord, saying, "Christ is my Pilot." When we stopped in Panama, I met up with three young people who were going to study in the same institute. I was comforted to meet with companions of my denomination who shared the same goal of serving our Savior. We arrived at the Bible Institute in San José and were received enthusiastically, as if we were sons who had been a long time gone from home.

A couple by the name of Thompson was in charge of the male students. The woman, Pearl, was like a second mother to us all. Her husband, William, was a gentle and caring teacher who, with his fatherly love, made us feel we were at home away from home. This, in turn, helped us in our training. On

Saturdays, we ventured onto the streets of San José to practice what we had learned about evangelism.

On my first day of practical work, I did as I had done in the early days of my conversion; I handed out tracts to people and then, right away, I withdrew from them. But my fellow evangelist taught me that it was necessary to talk to people and to show them how they might be saved. On Sundays, we traveled to a nearby village to evangelize. The administrators of the institute gave us no money to get to these places. When I had nothing with which to buy my necessities, I usually walked to the village, and in the afternoons, I walked back home again. That way, I was able to save for my personal needs. Getting around on foot was never a waste of time because along the road we always stopped at homes to share the Gospel and leave Christian literature. As a result of these contacts, we organized Bible studies for adults and children in the area. After a few years, churches were organized in each of these places.

Activities During Vacation

During the three months of vacation, I was sent with another colleague to any one of the six provinces of Costa Rica. On two occasions, we were assigned to the province of Guanacaste. I began to practice preaching, and in one small town, I preached several evenings. One couple attended those meetings every night. The woman was converted, but her husband resisted the message. I was praying for him, and I prepared a message with that man in mind. On the night I preached especially for him, he went to sleep – right from the moment I started! And although I pounded on the podium to arouse him, he didn't wake up until the end of the service. The attitude of this man taught me that the conversion of sinners does not depend on the strategy of the preacher, but on the power of the Holy Spirit. So I prayed for him and asked the Lord to touch his heart. The next night this friend returned, and the Lord moved upon his heart and forgave his sins.

The following evening a man came to the meeting who was an enemy of the new convert. After the service, the man who was saved the previous night went out quickly and waited for him. When he came out, the new convert asked forgiveness for the wrongs he had done. The two forgave each other, and shook hands. In that way, this new Christian demonstrated the change wrought in him through accepting the Lord as his Savior.

Another interesting incident during my vacation days in Guanacaste Province happened when my coworker and I were staying in the center of the town of Cañas, from where we evangelized outlying areas. One morning a man came to our room, and said, "I want you to come to my house to tell us about the Gospel." He told us that two years earlier he had bought a Bible, and that he and his family had devoted themselves to reading it, but they had never heard anyone explain it. Nor had they ever attended an evangelical church or known any evangelicals. We set the date for him to come and take us to his home. When we were parting, I said, "Let us pray that we will be able to make the trip and that it will be a blessing to all." Right away he said, "Do you want me to pray?" We answered, "Yes, please pray." I thought that this man, who had not even been to an evangelical meeting, would not know how to pray. But he prayed very intelligently, like someone familiar with evangelical Christianity. I was quite surprised by his ability to communicate with the Savior.

On the appointed day, this good man came to take us to his home. After three hours on horseback, we reached his place, a very humble house at the entrance of the village called La Cofradía. He had a wife and three children, and they were all keenly waiting to hear some exposition from the Scriptures. There in his house, he told us how the Lord Jesus Christ had done many miracles in his life through simple readings of the Holy Bible. He had stopped drinking. Previously, when he was very drunk, he would go out with a machete in hand, ready to fight with anyone. People locked their doors to prevent him from coming in and doing harm. But, through reading the Bible, he had learned that drunkards will not inherit the kingdom of God. And he had also stopped using tobacco, without anyone counseling him about it.

As well, this man had stopped eating sand. His house was on the edge of a creek of clear water which had fine white sand at the bottom. He ate it because, for him, it was sweet. His eighteen-year-old daughter had learned from her father to eat sand too. But she and her father learned what it says in 2 Corinthians 6:16: "You are the temple of the living God." Both of them were taught by God that eating sand and using liquor and tobacco are vices that offend Him and harm the body, which is God's temple. These basic lessons had remained with them ever since.

During our four days at the house of this brother, he and all his family surrendered their lives to the Lord Jesus Christ. Many who lived on the outskirts were also converted. Today a church organized by the Costa Rican Association of Bible Churches[1] serves all that area. These experiences helped me know how to preach effectively. I learned that we must wait on the Holy Spirit to do the work we cannot do and that we should wait for the Bible to speak for itself to those who hear it.

Marriage and Return to Colombia

Upon completing my three years of study at the Bible Institute, I had planned to go back to Colombia and start serving the Lord in the same church where I began my Christian life. But our plans are often not God's ways for His children. I had expected to return alone, but I pleaded with the Lord that, if it were His holy will and would be in His purposes, He would provide me

The wedding ceremony for Pedro Gutiérrez and Fanny Hogg was held in Costa Rica on November 26, 1937

with a suitable wife who shared my missionary vision. In the last year of my studies, I was particularly drawn to a young woman named Fanny Hogg. She was a nurse at the Christian Clinic who had graduated from the Faculty of Nursing at the University of Costa Rica. The Lord knew I needed someone just like her. He led us to love and understand each other and to share the same missionary vision. Our wedding took place in the chapel of the Bible Institute the same day we were to travel to Colombia. It was officiated by the director of the Latin America Mission, Dr. Harry Strachan.[3]

In 1937, the Latin America Mission sent two lady missionaries to begin an evangelistic outreach in the state of Bolívar on the northern coast of Colombia. There was only one small Presbyterian Church in this state, so two million people there had not read the Bible and knew nothing of the Gospel.

Before leaving Costa Rica, my wife and I promised God and the Latin America Mission that we would serve in that region of Colombia. Prior to going there, however, we visited my family near Albania in the state of Caldas. From there we traveled down the Magdalena River to the port of Magangué in the state of Bolívar. Then, from Magangué we traveled to Sincelejo by truck on a road that was only passable in summer.

Evangelization in Sincelejo and Beyond

In January 1938, we started our ministry in Sincelejo, the second largest city in the state. No evangelical Christians were to be found in the city, but there were some discouraged Adventists. Their leader had disgraced himself, and this was known all over the city. Every day I went out evangelizing with a fellow named Manuel Diaz, who was also a graduate from the Bible Institute in Costa Rica.

During his ministry trips in those days, Don Pedro traveled a lot by horseback

Because the people had rejected the Adventists, we found it difficult to evangelize. We had to explain to each family that we were not Adventists, that we kept Sunday, and ... "Yes, we ate *chicharrones!*" (fried pork rind). Week by week the Lord touched the hearts of people, and they were converted. These new believers asked us to teach them more, but since we did not have appropriate instruction manuals for them, I wrote several question-and-answer pamphlets. These were helpful in teaching new converts because, back then, 70 percent of the population could neither read nor write. Using these means, in the first year we had a congregation of more than 20 people. Dr. Harry Strachan performed the first baptisms.

From Sincelejo, every two weeks, I visited villages such as Corozal, Ovejas, Chalan, Palmitos and Zaban. On those trips I took Bibles, New Testaments, and explanatory tracts. When possible, I had meetings in the homes to teach the Bible to families and their neighbors.

First Miracle in My Body

One afternoon around 2 p.m., I came to the village of Palmitos. The sun was strong, and I was very thirsty. At one house I asked for a glass of water. They gave me cold water, but it was from a well in their back yard. I drank it very gladly. After three days evangelizing there, I went back home to Sincelejo, but two weeks later I had the first symptoms of typhoid fever.

In Sincelejo there was only one doctor, and at that time they had no penicillin to treat infections. The doctor gave me sulfathiazole pills, but the fever persisted. By the 19th day, I felt very weak. One evening, around 7 p.m., I started bleeding from my nose, and it would not stop. Someone went to call the doctor, but he was at his farm several hours away. I was getting weaker

Don Pedro's advice to pastors where churches have construction programs: "Never take charge of building projects"

by the moment, and I felt a ringing in my ears as if my life was about to end. Around 9 p.m., after two hours of bleeding and my condition having become very serious, Fanny knelt down, laid her hands on my head, and prayed, "Lord, put Your healing hand on Pedro. Stop the bleeding; cause it to cease, and grant that, by Your great power, he be restored to health." She pleaded before God with all her strength, and I, too, begged God that He would have mercy on me. After praying, I felt God's healing miracle. The blood stopped instantly, for He was doing His mighty work. That night, I was very sure that God had healed me. I spent 10 days with a slight fever, and then it left me completely.

The Beginning of the Evangelical Work in Montería

Between Sincelejo and Montería, there was a road that was only suitable for small vehicles in summertime. Since no air service existed then, one could only get to Montería during winter by the River Sinú. In Montería we found two Christians who belonged to the Presbyterian Church in Cereté. They could not attend any meetings because there were none in the city, so these believers offered their house for us to have Bible studies. After two weeks of going house to house to evangelize, additional new believers wanted to learn more about the Bible. By the end of the first month, 15 people were attending our meetings, and at the end of the year, the first believers were baptized by Dr. Harry Strachan.

With these baptized believers, we were able to organize the church and appoint deacons, deaconesses, a treasurer, and other leaders. Within five years the Mission purchased land, and some years later a spacious chapel was built, along with several rooms for church activities, including a grade school that served many children from Christian families and those of other faiths.

The Congregation in Montería

Chapter 2

New Congregations

Every month I traveled out from Montería to visit neighboring villages and to organize new congregations. At this time, the church in Montería required mature oversight of the Sunday services, the prayer meetings, and the visitation program. Fanny was the only person who could help me in the church. Besides graduating as a nurse, she had studied several pertinent Bible Institute courses in Costa Rica, so she was quite competent to teach the Bible to the adults and children. Therefore, when I was traveling, she led the prayer meetings and gave the Bible message on Sundays. She also taught lessons on nursing to several young believers whom she selected out of the congregation. She showed them how to give injections, how to attend to mothers after childbirth, how to sew and embroider, and how to handle their domestic responsibilities. Fanny also played the portable organ for worship and organized choirs and ensembles. She was in charge of special Christmas programs for the church and for other congregations, such as that in San José del Totumo. She did all this in addition to caring for our two children who were young and required special attention.

She was indeed a true helpmeet for me and for the Lord's cause. I constantly praise my Savior for Fanny.

Adventures in San José del Totumo

San José del Totumo was a village three hours on horseback from Montería that I visited once a month. The first time I was there, I went to the Pérez household. Four families in this area were meeting together in a home. At first, I spent three days with them, explaining the Scriptures in the daytime and teaching at night. They were illiterate; only one man, Víctor Velázquez, could read and write. To make myself understood, I had to use questions and answers with constant repetition. They eventually understood salvation and accepted the Lord as their Savior.

All these folk asked that they be taught something from the Bible on Sundays because they did not work that day, and they also wanted the children to have Bible lessons. To teach them on Sundays, I appointed Brother Víctor Velázquez, and I gave him a manual to study and use. This brother was keen to do something for the Lord, but a problem arose: he lived in cohabitation with a woman and their four children. I consulted with the missionary in Montería who was in charge of the Mission. She said I should not appoint someone as a Bible teacher who was not legally married. In these villages there was not one married couple.

I did not want to suspend the classes, because the teacher, as well as all the students, both adults and children, were being instructed from the Word of God. That year the Bible manual, which I was using every Sunday, had a series of studies on marriage. This brother had to teach the congregation about the sin of living in adultery and fornication.

One day he came to my house and said, "Brother Pedro, this past Sunday I had to teach about the sin of living in fornication and concubinage. Those who were there said to me: 'If you teach this as it is in the Bible, why don't you get married?'" And then he added, "I want you to arrange my marriage this very week."

To have a civil marriage ceremony was not feasible because the judges had never conducted one, and they were afraid of criticism by the priests of the Roman Catholic Church. After several months, the Lord helped us triumph over all the difficulties. We had a formal civil marriage, and later, a religious ceremony in the presence of the congregation. After this, many weddings were conducted there, and the church was established firmly and powerfully.

The Congregation in Planeta Rica

Planeta Rica, in the state of Córdoba, is located where the road from Montería joins the main route from Medellín to Cartagena. I first came to this town with a young man from Guatemala whom the Bible Institute in Costa Rica sent to us during the summer vacation to help evangelize the northern coastal area of Colombia. Neither of us was familiar with the road to Planeta Rica, but God directed us in a wonderful way. When we were still about two hours away, a friend joined us and accompanied us to the town and even took us to his house. His name was Delfín Garcés. He had heard the Gospel in Montería, and had once invited me to visit his home in Montería so that his family could learn about the Gospel.

In Planeta Rica we met a man named Robinson Arroyo. He had some knowledge of the Bible and offered his home as a place to meet. Every three months, I traveled there to evangelize and conduct services. Later, a small congregation was organized in Planeta Rica, and it prospered. Today, a large church thrives in that town, and the Gospel has penetrated the whole region.

Crossing the Carolina River

To get to Planeta Rica, I had to cross the Carolina River twice, but during the rainy season, this became impossible. On one of my trips from Montería to Planeta Rica, I found the river at flood level. I tried to cross it, but when I was midway, the horse pulled back, and I couldn't get it to walk any farther. Turning around, it fell in the river and I had to hold its head up to keep it from drowning. For about 15 minutes, I held the horse's head up. It trembled as if suffering from an acute cramp, but I managed to get it to stand up. All my clothes were soaked, and the Bibles and New Testaments were wet. The horse had responded, but what was I to do? There wasn't a house anywhere nearby where I could spend the night.

Leaning against the horse, I called out to the Lord, "What do I do, Lord? I can't turn back and I can't go on, and there's not a house nearby to where I can go. What should I do, Lord?" At that moment a man in the garb of a peasant appeared. I asked him, "What should I do, sir? How can I cross this swollen river?"

He replied, "Follow the riverbank, and four kilometers downstream, you will see a wooden bridge. You can cross there, and you will find your way to Planeta Rica."

I thanked him, and followed a path that seemed seldom used for it was almost overgrown. I arrived at the bridge and noticed that the gangway was only about four inches above the swirling water level. I dismounted, and went forward leading the horse carefully. The bridge was missing some planks, but the horse was careful to step over those gaps until it reached the other side.

I gave thanks to the Lord for His desperately needed deliverance at that river crossing. But, who was the man who guided me? I'm sure that it was the Lord Himself, dressed as a peasant, who helped me. Possibly, I was the last person to make it over that bridge. This was one other miracle that I saw in my service for the Lord. I praise Him because all my life He has come to my aid and has guided me on my way.

The Congregation in Providencia

Providencia is located in a jungle area of Bolívar state. When I was working in this area, most of the inhabitants were people who had fled to escape punishment by the law for wrongs they had committed back home. They entered the jungle and settled there. Police agents never appeared in the area for fear of being attacked. The government of Sahagun, the county seat of that township, gave orders to burn Providencia down. But no one ever dared, and I always thought this was to allow time for the Gospel light to shine on that place.

Brother Dolphin Garcés accompanied me on my first visit to Providencia. I stayed at the house of a man named Gil Santamaría who served as the inspector of police. In the square there was a small shop which, in the evenings, was lit by a gasoline lamp. I asked the shop owner to let me use a corner of his home, and also his lamp, so that I could preach the Gospel. He gladly let me do so, and said I could use that corner for whatever I desired.

At 7 p.m., I stood in the corner under the light, and began singing to attract the attention of some who were near. When I saw about 10 people around me, I started reading 1 John 1:7. Over and over, I repeated the words: "The blood of Jesus Christ His Son cleanses us from all sin."

A few minutes later another group came, and I again began my message. I did that three times until a fair number of listeners were gathered for the address. Then I reiterated these vital truths:

> We should acknowledge our sins, we should confess them to the Lord, and we should believe that the blood of Christ cleanses us from all sin.

That night I felt a great burden in my soul for these people who had never heard the Gospel. I slept in a room next to the street. The following morning, about 5 a.m., a man knocked on the door and said, "Mister, sell me one of those books that says, 'The blood of Jesus Christ His Son cleanses us from all sin.'" I opened the door, and sold him a New Testament for 25 centavos. I showed him where that text was and folded the page so that he could find it easily. He said he was leaving then for the San Jorge River where his family lived, and he would teach them from this book. I prayed for him before he left.

Several years passed before I found out that the man to whom I had sold the New Testament was Víctor Landero. He had shared that New Testament with his family and neighbors, had devoted himself to the study of the Scriptures, and had purchased Bibles in Montería and Sincelejo. The result of the New Testament sold that morning in Providencia was the salvation of many souls and the founding of several churches along the San Jorge River. The church in Providencia was established, and out of it, pastors and leaders were raised up for God's people.

The Congregation in Las Claras

Far up the Sinú River at the mouth of the Las Claras River, a Christian family owned a farm. The father of the family came to Montería where I was serving as pastor of the church that I had founded at the beginning of my ministry many years before. This brother asked me to come and visit them – people who knew the Gospel and wanted to learn more about the Bible. To get from Montería to Las Claras, one has to travel partway by bus, and then another day by boat on the Sinú River. When I first came to this place, a good group of interested people were waiting for me. They had a keen desire to understand the Word of God, so I was there three days teaching them and holding Gospel meetings every night. Because this was a farming community, many people came from a distance. As yet, there were no population centers in the area, even though some houses were already being built in what was to become a mainly Christian town.

I made the trip to Las Claras every three months. The believers were faithful, and they were interested in moving ahead spiritually. Given their fervent commitment, a farm owner, Mr. Manuel, offered a piece of land to build a meeting place. So they built a chapel that seated about one hundred people. Using timber from their farms, they made benches, and they built guest accommodation so that the pastor, during his travels, would have a place to stay. Two of the believers were instructed in how to teach the Bible, and these faithful Christians gathered every Sunday to worship the Lord and to study the Word of God.

This was a congregation that, with the care of the Great Shepherd and the loyalty of all the believers, really grew, for indeed the Holy Spirit was powerful in that place. On one of my visits, a man who lived quite a distance from the chapel came in. He was obviously determined to not allow himself to be convinced by the preacher, nor by anybody else. He tied his horse near the chapel and entered the meeting. He was attentive, like one who wanted to know what was said so as to oppose and reject it. But the Lord touched him powerfully, convincing him concerning sin and righteousness and judgment. He opened his heart to the Lord and truly surrendered himself to Christ. The next night this man returned, and he told the congregation how the Lord had convinced him of his sins, that now he felt he was a new creature, and that he had promised to be faithful to the Lord until death. We thank the Lord; He is able to convince the hardest heart.

Transferred to Cartagena

The Mission moved us to Cartagena, the capital of the state of Bolívar. There I had the opportunity to serve in two churches. One of them, called The Good Shepherd, was a new congregation that needed constant pastoral help. The other was called The Evangelical Temple. The Lord helped me to win souls there; they were genuinely saved through the blood of Christ. From Cartagena I traveled frequently, taking the Gospel to nearby towns.

The Congregation in Pasacaballos

This is a town two hours by bus from Cartagena. I traveled to Pasacaballos every two weeks, often by bicycle, but the heat was intense. In this village several people were converted, and one of them offered his home for the Sunday and weekday meetings. Many people attended those services. Two people were given training to lead services and to teach the Word. I hope the Cartagena churches have continued to serve these small congregations and that they continued to grow.

Transferred to Magangué

After several years of ministry in Montería and Cartagena, we were transferred to Magangué, a town located on the banks of the Magdalena River in the state of Bolívar. A small congregation already existed, which was started by missionary Robert Spencer with the collaboration of several colleagues. They evangelized the towns along the main river. We had the opportunity to serve the

The city of Magangué on the Magdalena River (1000 kms. navigable)

Lord in Magangué for eleven and a half years. I dedicated a lot of my time to door-to-door evangelism and holding meetings in various sectors of the city. This resulted in many people coming to the services, and there were numerous conversions among them. This population center presented unique opportunities to serve people and to organize congregations.

The Congregation on Isla Grande

Downriver from Magangué is a large island formed by the Magdalena River. Many of the inhabitants worked in agriculture. Some of them heard the Gospel and became genuine Christians. After their numbers increased, they decided to build a meeting place. They used timber brought in from the mainland and special island palm for the roof. The chapel served primarily as a place of worship, but many unevangelized people who wanted to hear the blessed Gospel felt welcome to come too.

On this island the Lord made His power known to us by a miraculous healing. A ten-year-old girl who could not swim was bathing in the river with other children. Suddenly, she sank into the mud. Her friends pulled her out, but she could scarcely breathe. We all prayed to God for her life, and He answered our prayers. She was able to breathe again normally. The Lord saved that little girl from a watery grave. This miracle drew many to seek the Lord. Sometime later, when the river level rose unusually high,

The Herald - used in the outreach to river populations

the chapel there was destroyed. The entire island was flooded, which ruined the island's agriculture and economy and forced the islanders to abandon their farms and their possessions.

The Congregation in Barranca

Barranca is an hour and a half by road from Magangué. With God's enablement, I organized a congregation of believers there. They were sincerely interested and met together on Sundays. I went there every two weeks to instruct them in the Scriptures, to teach them how to pray, and to prepare them with our catechism classes for baptism.

In Barranca, as I did in every other place, I trained leaders so that they could take charge of the administration of the congregation, teach the Bible, and preach in the normal services. In this way the meetings did not stop when I was not able to be there, and the leaders were better prepared with the teaching in the manuals I brought for them. In the Magangué church itself, I had six leaders who could preach when I was absent. The Lord blessed the church by using its own members to spread His message.

Pedro piloting the launch during river evangelism

The Congregation in Ayapel

Ayapel is a town located in the south of Córdoba state. From there, one day, a mother and daughter came to Magangué on business. They stayed at the home of a Christian family who brought them to church the following Sunday. This mother and her daughter bought a Bible, and I taught them some lessons from the Gospels. I also gave them instructions on how to use the Bible. When they returned to Ayapel, the whole family devoted themselves to the study of the Word of God, but they had nobody to teach them. I knew no more about this family until five months later. The mother and daughter came to Magangué again. The following Sunday they attended church.

As an offering to the Lord, they brought several thousand pesos that all the family had collected. They explained that by reading the Bible, they had learned to give God offerings and tithes of what He had given them. The mother of the family gathered them all together every Sunday. She had her daughter read the Bible to them, since she was the only one who had attended school; so naturally, she became the teacher of her siblings.

On one occasion, they asked me to go to Ayapel to encourage the whole family in their faith for they had no preacher. Travel to Ayapel from Magangué took three days by boat on the San Jorge River, or one could travel there by plane. They bought me a plane ticket to Ayapel and promised to meet me at the airport. They did keep their promise, and then took me to their house, where I stayed for several days. During this time we had meetings at night. In the daytime I taught them how to best use the Bible and did what I could to give them a general outline of the Gospel and some basics in doctrine. The Ayapel church grew and became numerically strong and stable in the faith. Miss Olinda Acevedo was the one who taught them, and through her own studies of the Bible, she herself acquired more knowledge. She had the gift of evangelism and shared the Gospel with everybody she met.

Don Pedro planted churches, counseled believers, and officiated at innumerable congregational events

Attempted Abduction of Pedro Luis

My son Pedro Luis completed his grade school studies in San José, Costa Rica, where he lived with his grandparents. This was a very profitable time for him because his grandparents and the aunts and uncles liked him a lot. However, for his high school studies, we decided he should live with us in Magangué. We enrolled him in a high school directed by a good and fair-minded man. But the professor of religion was a priest from the state of Boyacá; he was very sectarian and a fanatical opponent of evangelical Christians. Soon people knew that my son was not Catholic and therefore was ignorant of Catholic traditions.

One day, knowing that Luis was not baptized in the Roman Catholic Church, the priest got a student to tell him some things contrary to the evangelical faith and incited him to deceive his parents. He told Luis to get permission from us to go with them one Saturday to see the city, and they would take him to the "church." There, wealthy friends who could give him a lot of money would sponsor him. Also, on being baptized, they would send him to study in another city where we, his parents, would never find him, and he would become somebody important. They told him that by staying with us, he would never amount to anything because the evangelicals were of no consequence and were not recognized by the government.

Thank the Lord that little Luis was already a God-fearing Christian and had great confidence in us. That day, when he came home and told us everything his classmate had said, we understood that the priest planned to baptize him, kidnap him, and take him out of the city and possibly out of the country.

We were deeply concerned for our son. Every day after that I accompanied him to school and brought him home. We were very watchful of him. It all gave us plenty of reason to cry to the Lord for the future of our children, for we lived under clerics who were capable of unthinkable evil. This was the worst experience I had throughout my years of ministry. During this very distressing time, Luis finished his third year at the school, but he could not continue to study there. It was a year of agony and of constant prayer to the Lord. Then He answered our prayers in a surprising way.

That same year, an American appeared in Magangué. The government of Colombia hired him through what was called the INA, the National Agricultural Institute, to build silos for storing grain. This man and his wife were Christians, and they came to our church every Sunday to hear the Word of God. He learned about Luis' educational need, and, without our saying anything, he promised to pay for Luis to study at the American High School in Barranquilla.

The next year, I went to Barranquilla and talked to Pastor Juan Libreros who ran a hostel for students in his home. He accepted Luis, and I enrolled him in the American High School. He continued studying there until he graduated. Every month this American friend sent tuition money and, occasionally, an allowance to buy books and clothes. When Luis completed his studies there, this donor ceased communicating with us. Although we never heard any more of him, we never tire of thanking God for the help given to us at that particular time.

Plan to Assassinate Pastor Gutiérrez

Thirty couples and their children attended the church in Magangué. I performed 45 weddings there, but only five of the couples were young men and women. The other couples had lived in cohabitation. We saw the attendance increase to 300 people in the normal service, and about half attended the prayer meetings.

One Sunday a new couple came to the worship service. They returned several times and showed an interest in continuing with us. But later the woman came by herself and soon after, wholeheartedly gave her life to the Lord. Her conversion was genuine. The next day she came to our house to share her concern with us. She said that because she had accepted the Lord into her heart, she could no longer live with this man. He was married to someone else but had been with her for several years. His life was anything but good, so she had decided to leave him and move in with her mother. After two days she came to say goodbye. She already had her plane ticket to Barrancabermeja where her mother lived. She had planned the trip without telling him. She had only told him about how impossible it was to live with him since it was a great sin. She asked us to remember her in our prayers and left. We never saw her again. When the man she was living with realized that she had gone, he became very angry, not only against her, but against the pastor of the evangelical church. According to him, we were to blame for her having left him.

Rev. Pedro and Fanny Gutiérrez in the sanctuary of the first church in Magangué

Two months went by, and one day when I was visiting the believers, I came across this man in one of the homes. He called me over and told me that in the days after the woman had gone, he had thought about killing me. He said he had bought a gun and bullets for that purpose. He went and got drunk so that he would be more disposed to go to the church and kill the pastor. On the way, he met a friend. The man told his friend that he was going to kill the pastor of the evangelical church because he had advised the woman to leave him. The friend said, "Don't do such a silly thing. If the woman has gone away and left you, it is because she doesn't want you. There are many better women than her here. You can get another one and not commit such evil." This man, though quite drunk, reacted, went back home, and abandoned his plan to kill me. He himself told me all this, so I took the opportunity to explain to him what God does in the lives of those who are converted to Christ and given over to Him. I invited him to come back to the church, but he never came. My wife and I were very thankful to the Lord for looking after us and for changing this man's plans.

My Second Marriage

Fanny, my first wife, was Costa Rican. As I mentioned before, she was a graduate from the University of Costa Rica and one of the first nurses on staff at the Christian Clinic in San José. After leaving Costa Rica, we served the Lord with the Latin America Mission in a work they had begun the previous year in Bolívar State, Colombia. Fanny was very competent and worked every day giving injections, attending maternity cases, and visiting patients. Her service as a professional made hers a veritable missionary outreach. Patients queried her about the evangelical faith. She often gave them Scripture portions and would sometimes ask me to come and explain the truth of the Gospel to her patients. When I was traveling, besides attending to our two children, Fanny took care of the congregation, giving Bible studies, and often preaching in the evenings. She accompanied me in this way for 35 years. Then the Lord took her into His holy presence, and I was left to serve alone. This happened when we were working at the Inter-American (SMI) Calle Cuarta Church in Bogotá for the Lord had called us to serve with that denomination (begun by One Mission Society).[2]

Two very lonely years went by. I did not eat well, and I was feeling really poorly. So the time came when I was convinced I could not go on alone. With all my heart I pled with the Lord, "O Lord Jesus, if You want me to keep going as a pastor, please grant me a suitable companion to continue with me in my ministry." Then He answered my petition: He introduced me to Teresa Lizarazo who was finishing her studies at the Escuela Normal in Cúcuta. In February 1975, we were married, and we continued serving the Lord in the Calle Cuarta Church. Teresita has had a multifaceted ministry, including teaching in the inter-American schools and churches, helping with the music, and leading church youth programs. Despite being very young, she understood my call to Christian service and was indeed the helper that the Lord had prepared and whom I so much needed. She has been able to excel in her studies, and has obtained a degree in Spanish from the University of Gran Colombia in Bogotá. I praise the Lord for blessing me with Teresita.

Teresa - A Helpmate Indeed

The Congregation in Zulia, Boyacá

Zulia is a village near Maripí in the state of Boyacá. It is six hours by road from Bogotá to the nearest stop on the remote bus route and then another two hours or so by horseback across mountainous terrain and rivers that are impassable in winter. Farther on is the scattered community of Guarumal, which was the location of the first Zulia church.

The evangelical work in this place began through a congenial peasant named Eulises Hernández. He and his God-fearing wife, Ofelia, used to tune in every day on their small shortwave radio to hear the preaching of the Gospel by Domingo Fernández and José Andrade Crespo over Trans World Radio.

They also heard the Gospel on The Voice of the Andes from Quito, Ecuador. Don Eulises' testimony is recorded below (See: "Saved from the Abyss of Death.")

The Eulises Hernández family home served as a meeting place for the first believers. The group made remarkable growth, and people walked long distances to hear the Word of God. I traveled from Bogotá to visit that congregation every three months and usually stayed with them for a week, during which I conducted Bible studies in the daytime and preaching services at night.

I selected several people to be leaders and instructed them in Bible study methods. I also taught them how to teach the Bible to others.

"... Baptizing them in the name of the Father and of the Son and of the Holy Spirit" (Zulia, 1981)

Before long, five people could instruct the rest of the congregation. We set up programs so that they would know when it was their turn to lead the prayer meeting, the Sunday school, and the Sunday night meetings. With the help of these leaders, the church functioned almost as if they had a pastor. We had baptisms and weddings. And we sent some of the young people to study at the OMS Peniel Bible Institute[2] in Cristalina, Antioquia. The believers have since built a fine chapel seating 200 people.

The church in Zulia has paid dearly for its witness. Enemies of the Gospel assassinated two of its active and promising young men. The congregation is located near the Muzo emerald mines.

Quite often in that region, drunkenness and rivalry among those involved with emeralds also led to killings.

"The conversion of sinners does not depend on the competence of the preacher, but on the power of the Holy Spirit." - Rev. Pedro Gutiérrez S.

Saved From the Abyss of Death

Eulises Hernández lived in the outskirts of Zulia. He was increasingly attracted to the Gospel when listening to The Voice of the Andes and Trans World Radio on his little radio. There was no doubt in his mind that he was hearing the truth. But he pondered how he could ever manage to get a Bible and really understand these glorious words while living as he did, in such a remote place where nobody knew the Bible and with very little possibility of obtaining a copy. He considered these teachings to be very beautiful, but beyond his reach. So Don Eulises just kept thinking of how he could get to find out more about this wonderful truth.

One day while cutting timber on his farm, a log rolled over on him and pinned him to the ground. In danger of dying right there, he cried out to the Lord from the depths of his being: "Lord God Almighty, I know that You can forgive us our sins and deliver us from danger. Forgive me all my sins, for I accept the sacrifice that my Lord Jesus Christ made for me. Deliver me from this log so that it will not kill me." Immediately, he felt the log moving and was able to get out from under it. Although he was injured, he had been saved from death, and it was then that Don Eulises first saw God's miracles in his life. He was filled with deep gratitude to the Lord, knowing that He had rescued him, forgiven his sins, and saved him from being lost. His gratefulness to the Lord overflowed, and his desire to study the Bible and learn more about the Savior intensified.

Eulises Hernández – an intrepid evangelist (1976, Guarumal - Zulia)

Sometime later, while listening to The Voice of the Carrare from the city of Vélez, he discovered that meetings to explain the Gospel were being held in the city of Moniquirá. Soon after, Don Eulises set out with his wife and nine other relatives. After two days of travel, they reached their destination. The first thing he did was to buy himself a Bible, and the group attended all the daytime and evening meetings.

At the end of that week the conference speaker, Joaquín Espinosa, an inter-American pastor from the state of Antioquia, announced that some believers were to be baptized. Don Eulises said to Pastor Joaquín, "I have believed in Christ. He saved me from death and eternal punishment. I want to be baptized." So he was baptized. There was no doubt about his salvation, nor about the salvation of five of his relatives who were baptized along with him.

This man returned home and became a true evangelist. He

invited his neighbors to come to his house every Sunday to study the Bible and pray. In less than a year, his home group had become the first Christian church in that region. In a few months, 10 more believers were baptized. They built a chapel for their meetings. The other baptized converts started a second church. Don Eulises has never since ceased to proclaim the salvation he experienced in his own life.

The Congregation in Guachetá, Cundinamarca

Guachetá is a town three hours by road from Bogotá. It is in a coal region, and most of the workers there are employed in the mines. Víctor Novoa, who lived out there, had heard something of the Gospel and owned a Bible but was not a born again believer. Over Trans World Radio, he listened to an OMS program, The Acceptable Time, featuring Evangelist Eduardo Fiorenza. The program offered Bible studies entitled "Light of Life" that were based initially on the Gospel of John. At that time, I was associated with this radio outreach to the peoples of Latin America. In our Bogotá office, we dispatched and corrected the lessons and mailed answers to listeners' questions. Víctor Novoa wrote requesting more material and asking us to visit him at his home near Guachetá. He wanted to know more about the Bible. We set up a day, and I traveled out there with a young man from the church where I served.

I didn't know anyone in that town, so I asked at the small bus station if they knew a Mr. Víctor Novoa. They said no. What should I do? Well, I prayed to the Lord for His blessed guidance, and then walked over to another corner of the square where a man was listening to music on his little tape recorder. I asked him if he knew Mr. Víctor Novoa. He replied that he did know him, but that he lived a good distance out of the town. He also told me that Víctor's brother lived in the town itself. The attention this man gave me seemed a little unusual; it was the hand of God directing our way. The people of Guachetá were very guarded in their dealings with strangers, and it was difficult to gain their confidence. I learned however, that God guides our steps when we are in His service.

As directed, we waited at the house indicated, and in about half an hour, Víctor came in with groceries that he had bought for his family. Despite never having been acquainted, our meeting was just as if we were two brothers who had not seen each other for many years. Arriving at his house, I learned that he had invited neighbors to hear the Gospel. This, for them, was the first time. After the meeting that Saturday night, they asked me to continue visiting them and to bring Bibles, because they had never read a Bible. I invited them to return at 10:00 the next morning, and I would give them more teaching from the Word of God. Precisely at 10 a.m., other people joined those who had attended the night before, and so, we had the first Sunday school of a new church! I returned to Guachetá every month to explain the Word of God. Soon we organized for services to be held every Sunday and prayer meetings on

To reach his appointments, Don Pedro often had to travel along very dangerous rivers and roads

Wednesdays. This same brother, Víctor Novoa, took charge of leading and teaching in these meetings.

The congregation of Guachetá kept growing, and continued to meet in Brother Víctor's farmhouse. Some folks began attending from the surrounding countryside, and so the believers decided to centralize the meeting place in the town. A Christian family in Guachetá hosted these services. The believers put their offerings and tithes towards purchasing a property and the construction of a chapel. Land was bought, and in less than two years, they began to build a chapel seating 50 people.

Rev. Pedro Gutiérrez, Fernando Casas and Pablo Castillo contemplating the site of the future Guachetá chapel (1987)

A family, members of the Christian Fellowship Church[2] in La Víctoria, Bogotá, moved to Guachetá to give some leadership to the congregation. Then Guillermo Palacios, a young businessman in Bogotá who was converted and baptized in Guachetá, began traveling back there every weekend with Yolanda, his wife, and their family. They helped with the worship services, provided counseling, and made improvements to the chapel. God greatly blessed this church. A number of souls were saved, and

Guillermo served God for 24 years in the industrial world, and, with his family, as an OMS pastor in Bogotá

some members are taking the Gospel to other places. A student in Guachetá, Victor Casas, at his own expense, presented Christian films in several satellite communities and in his high school, where Guillermo had graduated earlier. He was the only professing evangelical in the school. Another convert, Fernando Casas, has given responsible and steady leadership to the church in Guachetá.

The "Emmanuel" Congregation in Bogotá

After spending two years serving in Miami, USA, at a church which was begun with Latino people (see page 53), my wife, Teresa, and I decided to go back to Bogotá to raise up a church in the sector where we had lived, Granada Sur. There, we found some believers who were like sheep without a shepherd. They wanted to organize a church in a neighborhood of over a million people. Bordering it were other sectors, like Veinte de Julio, without even one evangelical Christian church. We, and four believers who lived near us, decided to meet every Sunday at our home to worship the Lord and to study His Word. We saved our offerings and tithes to rent a meeting place, hoping eventually to have one of our own.

Very close to our house, we found and rented a suitable apartment for the meetings. Since we had no furniture, we agreed that each believer would buy a chair and donate it to the congregation. On Easter Sunday 1997, the group was organized as a church, and later we decided to name it "Emmanuel." This congregation saved their offerings to buy property and to build a chapel. Hernando Lombana and his wife Nina, a daughter of the congregation, became responsible for administering the church. They have started a group in the Belén sector and go there every Sunday to evangelize and teach the Word of God. The "Emmanuel" church, with God's help, may soon be strong and prosperous.

Reverence, order, and dignity were the consistent hallmarks of Pedro's ministerial life

Don Pedro with Eulises and Ofelia Hernández, son Marcos, and Jim Smyth (1998)

Chapter 3

Preparation of Leaders

In every church where I served, I prepared leaders to teach Sunday school and to conduct public services, as well as to preach in my absence. Of these, I will mention the following disciples:

Adam Gómez

As a very young man, Adam began attending the church in Montería along with his mother and siblings. I took him with me on my missionary trips and trained him to lead worship services and to teach the Bible. Because he had a keen desire to serve the Lord, we sent him to the Bible Institute in Costa Rica. He completed ministerial studies there, and on his return to Sincelejo, he married a fine Christian. They served together for a number of years pastoring a newly organized church in Calamar in the state of Bolívar. He was a successful pastor in several other congregations.

Manuel Hurtado

This young man was converted at 14 years of age on the farm of Dolphin Garcés. One of the daughters of Mr. Garcés taught him to read and write, for his heart's desire was to be able to study the Bible. He completed some courses at the Sincelejo Bible Institute, which was administered by the Latin America Mission. Later he was sent to the OMS Biblical Seminary[7] in Medellín where he grew in his knowledge of the Word of God. Upon his return he worked with me in Magangué, evangelizing and helping with Bible teaching in the church. He married Miss Cecilia Paternina, a member of the Magangué church. Manuel and his wife continued in the pastorate, and the Lord blessed him with glorious results in the salvation of souls. They are still faithfully serving the Lord.

Víctor Garrido

As a youth, Victor made his living by playing the guitar and singing at dances and festivals in Montería. He was also an artist whose paintings were widely popular. While employed in these different ways, he became ill. The doctor prescribed some injections for him. That was why he visited our house, for it was my wife, Fanny, who gave him the injections. Every time he came for treatment, Fanny would speak to him about the Lord, give him some Scripture portions, and invite him to come to the church services. Young Garrido did attend and became very interested in the music of the church. He came regularly until, one day, he was truly converted to Christ. After that, he accompanied me to evangelize and to hold meetings in the villages around Montería. He grew in Bible knowledge and proved very committed to helping others. Because of his keen desire to work for the Lord, he was sent to the Bible Institute in San José, Costa Rica. There he took particular advantage of sound instruction on how to preach the Gospel. On his return to Sincelejo, he proved to be a very good preacher.

Some years later, he went to study in the United States, and there he learned the art of presenting the Gospel through illuminated paintings. He did this to God's glory and, as a result, had a lot of invitations to use this method of teaching back in Colombia. Through this means, many souls were won to the Lord. Víctor married an American missionary in Cartagena, and together they pastored churches in the states of Bolívar and Córdoba. After several years of service in Colombia, they continued their ministry in the United States.

Luis Sepúlveda

Luis would have been about 15 years old when he showed up at our house in Montería. He had come overland from the state of Antioquia and then by boat on the River Sinú to reach Montería. He knew that there was an evangelical church in Montería, and he sought us out. He had left his parents and family to work as a commercial traveler. He would stay with us, and after finishing his business in the city, he returned home. He came every three months to Montería and always stayed in our home. This gave us the opportunity to help and guide him in his life. One day, he surrendered himself to Christ and was truly converted. Later, he manifested the Lord's call to serve Christ and felt that he should prepare himself. Therefore, we sent him to study at the Bible Institute in Costa Rica.

After finishing his studies, he came to Cartagena to work with the Latin America Mission. He served several years in the states of Bolívar and Córdoba and was able to give valuable help to the churches throughout that region of Colombia. He received an invitation to go to the city of Cali in the state of Valle and again was a real blessing to the church that he pastored there. Being an ambitious fellow, he moved to Nicaragua in Central America and, there too, served the Lord with great success. In Nicaragua he acquainted himself with a very special young Christian and married her. With her help, he became better organized and more stable in the pastorate. The Lord used him in large evangelistic campaigns in northern Colombia, in various Central American countries, and in Venezuela.

Freddy Lizarazo

Freddy is the nephew of my wife, Teresa. When he was still quite young, I helped him to develop his knowledge of the Bible. He was truly converted to Christ, and from that moment, he showed a desire to serve the Lord. He attended the meetings and always helped however he could in the church. After finishing high school, we encouraged him to attend the Biblical Seminary of the Christian and Missionary Alliance[5] in Bogotá, and while he was completing his theological studies, he preached in some of the Christian Fellowship churches. He led youth groups and was active in their Christian camps. The Christian Fellowship church in the Inter-American High School[6] appointed Freddy as their youth pastor.

Teenagers Freddy Lizarazo and Daniel Gutiérrez serve the Lord fervently in the "Emmanuel" church

Whenever we make a trip back to Bogotá from the United States, Freddy comes to my house every day with theological issues. He asks how to work with young people, about preaching methods, how to give the invitation to receive the Lord, and about many other matters related to the pastorate. From time to time, he brings potential young leaders to me so that I can answer their questions, give them advice on the Christian life, and talk to them about the call to active service in the church. Freddy is one of those who will replace me in my sacred ministry.

PREPARATION OF LEADERS

Pedro has always put special emphasis on thorough preparation of pastors and elders.

With God-given insight and wisdom, he devoted himself to the training of leaders.

Chapter 4

Attending to People in Special Need

"The Priest Heard Her Confession, so She's Ready to Die"

I went out one morning with my briefcase full of Gospel booklets. I had nowhere particular in mind, so at the first corner, I stopped a moment to ask the Lord to show me where I should go or who to visit. I walked on about five blocks and stopped at the next corner again to seek the Lord for His blessed guidance. While standing there, I heard several banging noises in a house nearby. I walked over there and found a woman arranging her living room. I asked her what was happening and if she needed any help. She said, "My mother will likely die today, so I am preparing the living room for her wake." I asked if I could come in and talk with her mother. She said, "Come on in and see her; she's in the other room." As she walked in, she kept saying to me, "Three days ago the priest came and heard her confession, so she's ready to die." When I saw the sick mother, I asked her, "Friend, are you sure that your sins are forgiven?" She said, "No. The priest came. I confessed my sins to him, and he gave me Communion. But I feel that my sins are not forgiven." I took the Bible, and read some passages about forgiveness of sins. Then I invited her to pray to God with all her heart for His forgiveness. She repeated the prayer that God would, through the blood of Jesus Christ, take away her sins and pardon her. Then I talked with her as to a person who does not have many hours to live. I asked her how she felt after sincerely asking for God's forgiveness, and she responded, "Now I feel that God has forgiven me."

I said goodbye to her, and the next day I came back at the same time. The daughter, when she saw me, said, "I was waiting for you, because my mother wants you to talk some more about her salvation." I asked the mother if she was indeed sure that she was saved. She told me that yes, she was sure of her salvation, but she wanted me to tell her something more about heaven. I spoke to her again about forgiveness and of being fully assured of going to heaven. For a long time I prayed with her, read to her, and talked to her about being sure of her salvation. The next day she died, and I accompanied the family to the cemetery. The following Sunday several of the relatives came to our evangelical church. I thank the Lord for leading me to that house.

"I Feel All Lightened Up"

A large family that attended our church in Montería frequently brought their grandfather with them. He was an old man and a little deaf. One day a member of the family came to our home at the church saying, "Brother Pedro, please come to our house and talk to my grandfather; he is very ill, and we think he is going to die." So I went as they requested. The grandfather's name was John. Because he had a hearing problem, I got close to him and read him Bible verses about forgiveness of sins. As best I could, I explained salvation to him - as to one who was hearing about it for the last time and who was soon to go out into eternity. I invited him to repeat with me the prayer for forgiveness, asking the Lord to save him, and I had him repeat it several times. Then I prayed for him, calling on the Lord to save him. However, when I finished praying, I felt a little concerned whether or not he had understood the matter of his salvation. Therefore, I said to him, "John, how do you feel after asking the Lord to forgive your sins?" He replied, "I feel all lightened up." When he said this, I knew that the weight of his sins had been lifted; he was at peace with God and ready to meet the Savior. I made several visits to see him after that. Each time, he affirmed to me that God had indeed forgiven his sins and that he was sure of his salvation. I know I'll see John in heaven, because his sins were forgiven.

"I Was Going To Drink This Poison"

One day a beggar came to our parsonage in Montería. When I saw him, the Lord Jesus impressed upon me that this man, in addition to needing money, needed God. We gave him some food and some money, but I invited him to sit down and listen carefully to the Gospel. I talked to him as if it were his last opportunity to be saved. I invited him to give his life to the Lord and led him in a prayer asking God for forgiveness. Then I pled with the Lord to save him, for a deep desire came over me to help this man. When I had finished praying, I talked a while longer to him, explaining matters related to his life and what God required of him. When I finished, he opened his little case and took out a bottle of liquid. "Look, mister," he said, "today I had planned that after talking to you I was going to drink this poison, but now I will not do it because God has forgiven me. He has saved me, and I understand that I must continue to live until He takes me into His presence." He gave me the bottle of poison, and I disposed of it where nobody would ever find it. This man came to church the following Sunday. Then he left

Montería, and I never saw him again. I am sure that God saved him and that he will enjoy heaven's eternal glory.

"Some Have Entertained Angels Unawares"

One morning, a man arrived at our home in Montería who had come to know the Gospel elsewhere. He was planning to go to Planeta Rica on foot. There was no road, so this would take him two days. From Planeta Rica he hoped to go by bus to Medellín and find an evangelical Bible school where he could study. His desire was to be a worker for the Lord. We fed him a good breakfast, prayed for him, and gave him some advice about the trip. Then we said goodbye.

After several years, I was visiting some congregations in Turbo, in Acandí, and in the region of Santamaría la Antigua del Darién. This was by invitation of the Inter-American Mission,[2] which had churches there.

When I finished that weeklong trip, I returned to Turbo for a campaign lasting several days. On the first night, a man came in who was very attentive to the message. When the service ended, he came to me, gave me a big hug and asked, "Brother Pedro, do you remember me?" I said, "I'm sorry, brother, but I can't remember you." He told me that he was the man who had once come to our house in Montería and whom we had helped with food and money for his journey to Planeta Rica. And that he had gone to Medellín and had prepared himself at a Bible institute there for the pastorate. His first appointment had been in Turbo, and the Lord had greatly blessed him in His labors. He thanked me over and over for helping him and promised to pray for me. That day I learned that this is what the apostle meant when he wrote, "Some have entertained angels unawares" (Hebrews 13:2).

ATTENDING TO PEOPLE IN SPECIAL NEED

"My Mother Wants You to Tell Her More About Jesus Christ"

One night in Magangué when I was on my way home, I saw a woman sitting on a roadside bench looking very worried and sad. I felt motivated by the Lord to go over and speak to her. I asked her, "What is wrong, lady? Are you sick?" She replied, "I'm just waiting here because my mother is dying; she has tuberculosis and for days now is getting worse." I asked her, "Where is your mother?" She pointed to a small hut and said, "Over there." I asked her to please take me to see her, but she didn't want to and told me that her mother could no longer speak. I persisted, saying I really wanted to talk to her mother about salvation before she died; so she took me into the shack. Her mother couldn't speak but was able to hear me and understood what I was saying to her. I explained the way of salvation very clearly to her and invited her to ask God for forgiveness for her sins. She knew what I meant, and I helped her in her very weak state as she repeated the prayer asking for forgiveness for sin and for cleansing by the blood of Jesus Christ.

The next afternoon when I was walking along that street, the daughter was there in the same place waiting for me. She saw me and said, "Mister, I'm here waiting for you because my mother wants you to tell her more about Jesus Christ." I stepped in to visit her and was surprised that she could speak to me quite clearly. She said she had peace now, because she knew that Jesus Christ had forgiven her. I had her repeat with me again the prayer for forgiveness. I assured her that she was saved because she believed in the Savior. The next morning I went to visit her, but she had already died. The neighbors had promptly taken her body to the cemetery. I did not see her again, but I am sure she is in heaven enjoying the salvation she received during her last two days of life on earth.

Death and Salvation in the Square

One Monday morning after finishing with the church meetings in rural Guarumal, I returned with a missionary named Keith Wonderly to the village of Zulia, Boyacá. In Zulia we found several men with shotgun wounds. One of these was in a serious condition. I prayed for him and then moved on. In the corner of the plaza, there was a man who had died. In another corner was a man who was mortally wounded. I got down from my horse and went into the house where they had carried him. He spoke faintly but could still hear me. I read the Word of God to him and invited him to repeat after me a prayer for forgiveness for his sins. I had him say it several times, and I continued praying for him that the Lord would grant him salvation. I asked him if he had understood and if he was sure that God had forgiven his sins. The dying man turned his head. In a very weak voice, he said yes, he had received forgiveness for his sins. About twenty minutes later, he passed away. After a short time, we left him, but I'm sure he was saved and that he is in the presence of the Lord.

Many people were led to the Savior through Don Pedro's conversations and prayers. He is pictured here in Zulia with the Eulises Hernández family, and neighbors

Idols Buried

Guadalupe Jaraba was a very poor woman. She lived in the city of Montería and earned a meager living by washing clothes. Her husband worked on farms, doing whatever the owners required of him. Both were practicing Roman Catholics, and they lived in a humble house with two small bedrooms. They occupied just one of the rooms for the other was filled with images and pictures of "saints" and all kinds of idolatrous stuff that Guadalupe had bought. They worshiped these things and burned candles for them every day.

Ours was the only evangelical Christian church in the city, and we systematically visited the homes with the Gospel. One day when I came to Guadalupe's house, I concentrated on showing her the plan of salvation. I explained to her the great love that Jesus Christ had shown towards her, even to the point of offering His life as a sacrifice for her.

Holy Week was approaching, and I invited Guadalupe to come and listen to the messages. She attended the meetings on Maundy Thursday, Good Friday, and Easter Sunday; but her husband stayed at home to look after their idols. On Good Friday the Lord touched her heart; she repented of her sins and promised the Lord that she would follow Him until death. That same day she bought a Bible and began to read it like someone satisfying an intense thirst for knowledge.

After a few weeks, I went to see Guadalupe and was surprised to discover that all the idols in their house were gone! "What happened to the pictures, Guadalupe?" I asked. Then, in a firm tone of voice, she told me this: "The Bible has taught me that adoring all those pictures we had was sinful and offends the Lord. Therefore, I smashed some of them and burned the others. I buried all of them in a deep hole so as to not offend my Savior again." Guadalupe spoke to her husband of the need to be saved. She brought him to church, and just as it had happened to her, he was converted. Both remained faithful to the Lord from that day onward.

The final hours of this Christian lady were the most beautiful of her life. In that humble house where they lived, Guadalupe became fatally ill. I went again to visit her scarcely twenty minutes before she died, and I asked her, "Sister Guadalupe, how do you feel now?" She spoke to me with real assurance and said, "I feel really well. Only a few moments ago the Lord came, and He said to me, 'I am coming for you soon.'" Twenty minutes after she had spoken those words, the Lord Jesus Christ returned and took her to His eternal glory.

The Blood

Humberto Ortega was a poor man who lived in one of the most underprivileged sectors of the city of Montería. He worked as a farm hand and heard his fellow laborers talking about several people who were killed by fanatical men who had become their enemies because of political differences. This made Humberto very fearful of what could happen to him and his family. One afternoon while walking home after heavy rain, he felt very worried. What might occur if the violence came to his neighborhood? Walking on along the street, he tried to sidestep the puddles and mud but couldn't avoid the muck and slime for there was no other way to get to his humble abode. Suddenly, in the slush he saw a scrap of paper with the word "BLOOD" printed in red. On seeing this, Humberto said to himself, "I wonder who they have killed now." He reached down for the torn piece of dirty paper and wiped it clean enough to be able to read these words: "THE BLOOD OF JESUS CHRIST HIS SON CLEANSES US FROM ALL SIN." As he pondered this text, Humberto thought: "It was the Lord Jesus Christ whom they killed." He wanted to read the whole tract, but it was practically destroyed. All he knew was that the Christians of the evangelical church in the city had distributed it.

The following Sunday, Humberto attended our church. He listened with keen interest to the teaching about the Person who had died for him. That next Sunday he accepted Jesus Christ into his heart as Savior and Lord. And so, what he had read about on that scrap of dirty paper was realized in his own life: "The blood of Jesus Christ … cleanses us from all sin." This poor man talked to his wife and children about salvation through the blood, and he shared the same message with his fellow laborers. From the moment he gave himself to Christ, the great fear he had lived with was gone. He committed his ways to the One who can free us from all evil and keep us at peace in times of violence.

Missionary Work in Miami, Florida, USA

Under the leadership of OMS missionary Roy McCook, the Inter-American Mission planted a Spanish-speaking congregation in Miami. He later came to Bogotá and invited me to join him in Miami to assist with that project. After we had prayed about it, my wife Teresa and I were sure it was the will of God for us to move there.

In July of 1987, we arrived in Miami and began to work among the Spanish-speaking population. The church prospered, and in the first two years, we had a congregation of over 60 people. Members were continually being added, and believers from Brazil and several Central American countries joined with us to worship God in that place.

God's anointing was on his servant Pedro Gutiérrez to the very end of his days

Part Two

Part Two

Chapter 5

"The Modest Giant From Quindío"

**A Biographical Supplement
By Jim Smyth**

The Reverend Pedro Gutiérrez was not only my senior by two decades, but infinitely ahead in piety. So for me, being permitted to complement his narratives with these few observations is a genuine honor. I am also aware that others, who have likewise been inspired by him in their service for Christ, could have gladly added their own treasured memories of our revered "Don Pedro."

First Impressions of a Beautiful Ministry

In 1969, I arrived from Northern Ireland to study Spanish for seven months at the Language Institute in Costa Rica. Fortunately for me, soon after settling in to learn in this very different culture, I met the Rev. Pedro Gutiérrez and his wife Fanny. They were pastoring the Latin America Mission "Berea" Church in the Monterrey sector of the capital, San José.

For a time, I lodged with a family of "ticos" in their tiny, humble dwelling. The father was a member of the church where Don Pedro preached and formed part of a trio that played stringed instruments. Accompanied by a pianist, they provided great music in the church. These self-taught guitarists were my introduction to Latin American music, and I greatly enjoyed their participation in the services. But I was especially blessed with the really clear articulation of the pastor in his preaching. I easily learned my first Bible verse in Spanish, which was engraved on the front of Don Pedro's pulpit: "Believe on the Lord Jesus Christ, and you will be saved, you and your household" (Acts 16:31). Soon I began to understand gradually the content of the lessons. Since that time, the sermons, the exemplary life, and the faithful ministry of Don Pedro have been a refreshing influence, and are sacred memories. I never cease to thank God for this pastoral couple and for our friendship back then. Much of the following is from notes Don Pedro had me record or from my own recollections of him.

Don Pedro and Fanny's ministry in this Costa Rican church made it a center of spiritual renewal

A Great Adventure Begins ...

Born on September 9, 1914, Pedro Antonio Gutiérrez Santamaría was the second son among the 13 children of Christopher and Griselda Gutiérrez. He began his official pastoral ministry in 1938, but in reality, he served the Lord from when he became a Christian at age 14. He was converted in his father's house near the town of Calarcá, an area of coffee plantations about five miles from the capital, Armenia, in the state of Quindío (formerly Caldas). Following his conversion to Christ, his life has been a fascinating pilgrimage. He never strayed from the ways of the Lord, and his story is of particular benefit to all who seek to please the Lord and want to dwell in God's holy place.

Segundo Pasminio, a colporteur of the Cumberland Presbyterian Church, visited that farming area and had meetings in some homes. Pedro and two other brothers went with their father to most of these gatherings. Other people came on horseback, and the benches they sat on were rough boards with bamboo padding. Among the more faithful attendees was the Barrios family. Segundo discipled one of the believers, Patricinio Cocuyí. When Segundo could not be there, he left Patricinio in charge of the Sunday morning services. The folk liked this fellow, and as Don Pedro told us in his narrative about the first Sunday school meetings, Patricinio provided cigarettes for them. Naturally, Pedro had learned to smoke along with the workers on his father's two large coffee farms. The leader did not yet have much knowledge of the Bible, but he was a good teacher. He counseled the people about the errors of the Roman Catholic Church.

Colombia is probably the world's best-known producer of fine coffee

One Wednesday evening, Martiniano Fajardo, a Cumberland Presbyterian preacher from Cali, taught a class on Romans 6:23, "The wages of sin is death, but the gift of God is eternal life." That night this Scripture deeply affected Pedro. At home, when his brothers had gone to sleep, he knelt in his room, asked forgiveness for his sins, and pled with God to make him His child. Right away he received the assurance that God had forgiven him. "Since then," he tells us, "Jesus has been my best friend." One of his favorite songs was "Even when I'm sad and tired, Jesus is my best friend…"

Despite being a timid boy and fearful of speaking in public, Pedro had a desire to serve the Lord, so he spoke about Christ to the workers. When he went to the weekly market in Armenia, he always distributed Bible tracts among the people. Between the ages of 14 and 18, he taught Sunday school, led the youth gatherings, and often helped the pastor with meetings in the homes and on the streets of Cali. At age 17, he was baptized in Cali by missionary David Brayson. After the Cumberland Presbyterian leaders came to organize the new work in those coffee plantations, Pedro told them of his aspiration to serve God.

As time went by Pedro was greatly encouraged by Pastor Martiniano Fajardo. He would hear Pedro preach and say, "Very good, Pedro," and then correct his use of words. Once, when he was preaching with Martiniano on a street corner, some youths disrupted the open-air meeting. Pedro stopped preaching, ran after them, and threw stones at them. Later, Martiniano asked him, "Why did you stop preaching?" and he replied, "To catch those fellows, and have them put in prison!" So Martiniano reproved him. Pedro was later elected president of the church's youth association. He gathered the young people together on Saturdays for instruction from the Bible. Among these were some of his own brothers. The congregation grew rapidly, so they began looking for a pastor, even though at this time, some families had moved to Central America.

"You'll Do!"

In those days, Pedro was praying about the possibility of studying at the Latin America Bible Seminary in Costa Rica. His father, Don Cristóbal, was aware of what was in his mind. But Pedro, now 18, had to resolve the issue of compulsory army service. So, Pedro went to the Buga military depot in Armenia. After being duly examined, a commander tersely told him: "You'll do!" He knew, therefore, he would have to either serve as a soldier or pay for the military card exemption. So he made this concern a matter of earnest prayer. Money was never the problem. His family had prospered in the coffee business. Pedro did not want to borrow money from his father for the card; he wanted to see God's hand in the whole matter.

God's affirmation of his plan to go to seminary came unexpectedly. A well-known evangelist who was visiting from Costa Rica told Pedro's father, "Don Cristóbal, it would be well worth it for your boy to go to seminary." After reflecting on this, his father gave Pedro not only the $250 pesos for the military card, but sufficient funds to obtain his passport in Cali and to purchase his ticket to San José, Costa Rica. So, in March 1934, Pedro traveled by ship from Buenaventura on the Pacific coast, through the Panama Canal, and into Puerto Limón on the Atlantic coast of Costa Rica. Then he traveled by train to the capital, San José.

Pedro was 23 when he graduated from the seminary in November 1937. The next day, a Saturday, he married Fanny, one of the nurses who made up the medical team at the Bible Clinic in San José. Fanny was qualified to serve in all branches of obstetrics, except surgery. In later years, her medical work in Colombia would become legendary.

An Ideal Couple in God's Work Together

Pedro and Fanny came to Colombia via Puerto Limón, Panama, and Buenaventura; then they traveled on to Armenia, where they visited his parents for a short time. After this, they began their ministry in his native land and worked together for the next 35 years. They pioneered in the states of Córdoba and Bolivar and helped to form what became the Association of Evangelical Churches of the Caribbean (AIEC)[1] – with more than eighty churches and many thousands of believers. They began in Sincelejo and then for approximately five years served in Montería. There they started a church and a school, and their two sons, Pedro Luis and Juan David, were born in Montería. While working there, Don Pedro established churches also in Planeta Rica, San José del Totumo, Providencia, and other centers. Fanny was a true helpmate in multiple ways. In Montería one would often hear folks say: "Yes, yes, Doña Fanny, our beloved nurse. It was she who helped usher me into the world!"

In those early years, Don Pedro often traveled on horseback in the carrying out of his responsibilities. Normally his itinerary lasted six days: four days on the trail and two days of ministry. One can scarcely imagine the challenges he encountered in the pastoral and evangelistic mission to open up much of northern Colombia to the Gospel. For example, the trip from Montería to Planeta Rica, which in later years took about 45 minutes by bus, meant two days on horseback. Aside from the hassles of the trail itself, there were the real dangers of criminals who stole horses and murdered lone travelers. On one occasion, after Dr. Strachan journeyed with him and became aware of the risks along the way, orders were given that on these mission trips Don Pedro should always be accompanied.

Harry Strachan

The Word of God is Not Bound

Don Pedro has earlier referred to his experiences in Providencia when he preached in public, and how one of his hearers, Víctor Landero, came to where he was lodging and bought a New Testament. But it was years later that Eliezer Benavides, a young man whom Don Pedro had led to Christ, arrived in Nueva Estación, the town where Víctor lived. In those places, the evangelist would usually ask people if they knew anybody there who read the Bible. Folks had seen Víctor as he sat in the evenings out on the sidewalk beside his house with his Bible, and they told Eliezer where Víctor's house was. He visited him, and after he explained some Bible verses to him, Víctor accepted Jesus Christ as his Savior. Around that time, Victor's parents, brothers, and many of his relatives were also converted to Christ.

In subsequent years, a number of the Landero family members played important roles in the Association of Evangelical Churches of the Caribbean. Víctor is an uncle of Loida Huertas who graduated in Medellín from the Bible Seminary of Colombia (SBC)[7] – where she met her husband, Luis Miguel. Together they pastored a mid-upper-class church in Bogotá, the Christian Fellowship, Unicentro. Luis Miguel was a top student at the Bogotá Inter-American High School. His life as an adolescent and his pioneer missionary career would constitute another extraordinary account. One of Víctor's brothers, Gregory Landero, became a long-term member of the Board of the Bible Seminary of Colombia. Dr. David Howard's book, "Hammered as Gold,"[8] relates other dramas of the Landero family and about those years in the life of Don Pedro.

Later, Don Pedro and Doña Fanny moved to Cartagena on the Caribbean coast and served there for several years. During this time they worked in two churches, one of which grew remarkably. It was during this period that they helped organize a hostel as well as schooling for several girls, which afterwards developed into what is now the Latin America High School of Cartagena.

"La Violencia"

It is a sad fact that the history of Colombia was marked for many years by intense hostility against the evangelical faith. Between 1948 and 1958, the nation suffered from the Violencia, a bloody conflict between the main political parties. The following, told to us by Don Pedro, helps put it in some perspective:

"In the year 1846, the British Consul was expelled from Bogotá by the Government and the Catholic Church because he was a foreigner who was an active representative of the British Bible Society. He was dispatched by mule to La Dorada, a port on the River Magdalena, with orders that he be taken to Barranquilla on the Caribbean coast: he never arrived. As for a consignment of Bibles that the Consul had brought to the capital, the Catholic Church stacked them up in the city's Plaza de Bolivar and burned them. Several years went by, and in 1920, Harry Strachan and James Thompson (an Englishman) came to Bogotá. They met with General Uribe and other high-level Colombian politicians. These men were determined that the Colombian people should have free access to the Bible. Regrettably, the Catholic Church arbitrarily forbade this liberty, insisting that the Bible must be read and interpreted only by the Catholic priesthood."

The hostility took many forms. When Don Pedro and Doña Fanny were administrating the school that they had founded in Magangué and were pastoring their church, authorities in the city imprisoned and tortured some of their Christian friends. Among those taken was the Rev. Joaquín Espinosa, a pastor of the Association of Inter-American Evangelical Churches of Colombia (SMI).[2] The reason given for their detention was: "They have preached the Gospel in Pinilla, Colorado, and

Rev. Joaquín Espinosa

several other towns in the region." When these were released from prison, Nurse Fanny attended to their wounds.

Don Pedro and Doña Fanny themselves suffered persecution for their Christian witness. While visiting villages along the River Magdalena with Luis Calderón, who often piloted El Heraldo, their Gospel launch, they were arrested and imprisoned. After two hours they were released, but were robbed of the Bibles they had planned to distribute. On another occasion, the Catholic priest of the city closed the school in Magangué. However, the students continued their studies in private homes until the problem was resolved. It was a harsh experience for the Magangué believers, but within a year attendance at the church had increased to 350.

Pedro Gutiérrez with some of his disciples[9] – 1942

After evangelization began in northern Colombia in 1937, the Association of Evangelical Churches of the Caribbean (AIEC) in Colombia grew significantly until the late 1960s. Don Pedro was prominent among the founders of the AIEC. He was its first president and held that office intermittently for eleven years between 1945 and 1958. For fourteen years he was a member of the Administrative Committee. He proved notably competent in formulating the denominational Statutes, writing its Bylaws, preparing its Manual of Discipline, and in giving oversight to doctrinal issues. In addition, on some occasions he was a platform speaker at Evangelism in Depth crusades and in Billy Graham Evangelistic Association campaigns, preaching in the cities of Panama, Colón, and Managua (Nicaragua), – reaching out well beyond his own Jerusalem, Judea, and Samaria.

New Challenges for the Modest Giant from Quindío

After an interlude of two years in Costa Rica, during which they pastored in Monterrey, San José, Don Pedro and Doña Fanny returned to Colombia in 1969. Their fervent desire was to continue preaching the Gospel throughout Colombia and to plant churches. However, the Lord showed Don Pedro that they should do so in partnership with a different Mission. For this reason, Don Pedro contacted the Christian and Missionary Alliance and the Inter-American Mission (OMS).

His first reply came from the Rev. Bruce Hess, field director of OMS in Colombia and founding president of the inter-American churches there. Rev. Bruce Hess consulted with the then president of the denomination, Rev. Felipe Barajas, and shortly thereafter Don Pedro became a pastor with the Inter-American Mission. He had been familiar with OMS after its 1943 debut in Colombia. On trips to the north coast, OMS missionaries often stayed at the Latin America Mission headquarters in Sincelejo and sometimes preached in the Sincelejo

For six years, Don Pedro pastored the Fourth Street church in the heart of Bogotá

and Cartagena churches. However, Pedro and Fanny had a more direct contact with OMS people when attending the popular Víctorious Life conventions on the OMS campus in Medellín, home of the Biblical Seminary of Colombia.

Rev. Pedro Gutiérrez was one of the founders of the Bible Society of Colombia and a valued member of its board for many years. He became a superintendent of the inter-American churches (now IGLEICO),[2] pastoring first in the city of Puerto Berrio for six years, then in two Bogotá churches, the Fourth Street Church for six years and later the Santa Lucia Church. It was during his pastorate in Santa Lucia that, in December 1972, his beloved wife Fanny died.

Don Pedro's vision was that "all the ends of the earth would see the salvation of our God" (Isaiah 52:10) As here, in Guarumal!

In February 1975, Don Pedro was married to Teresa Lizarazo in the Fourth Street Church. Teresa had been a teacher in the cities of Bucaramanga and Cúcuta for about two years; she then taught for two years in the Bogotá Fourth Street Church school and later in the Inter-American High School in Bogotá for six years. Don Pedro served on the High School board for twelve years. He was also significantly involved in the organizing of the Christian Fellowship congregation in La Victoria, south Bogotá, where his pastoral spirit and support were particularly appreciated by Rev. Rafael Villar, the leader of the church and school there.

While pastoring in Bogotá, Don Pedro collaborated with a radio ministry of OMS, "The Acceptable Time." He handled the communications generated by it and the Light of Life Bible courses used in conjunction. Through these means, he was able to evangelize and counsel listeners and students in several Latin countries. In addition, it was by this ministry that God used him in the founding and nurturing of a congregation in Guachetá. His dedicated labors during those years contributed to the consolidation of many new churches, including those planted by OMS in the cities of Duitama, Moniquirá, Garagoa, and distant Zulia. In some of these centers, Don Pedro was often invited to preach on local radio. During his later years, he served with amazing energy, especially in the Bogotá churches of Veinte de Julio, Country Sur, and Villa de los Alpes. Always an evangelist and a counselor to those around him, he organized yet another church, "Emmanuel," in Granada Sur, close to his small Bogotá residence.

"Good and Faithful Servant"

Reflecting on his eventful decades of life, Pedro Gutiérrez pondered why God chose him from among his brothers to preach the Gospel. His siblings prospered in various enterprises, including the local cultivation and commerce of coffee in the state of Quindío. But he confessed that, for him, it was better to suffer the disciplines of a servant in "the vineyard of the Lord" than to merely live contentedly in affluence and personal comfort.

Don Pedro's life as a minister of God was consistently praiseworthy. His unhesitating commitment to Christ and his diligence in the performance of his clerical duties impressed many. He was methodical, composed, and always gracious. His kindly disposition was manifest in his quiet forbearance and sincere compassion. Remarkable, too, was the ease with which he made friends of strangers, whether in the public square or in jungle remoteness. On his frequent and often arduous trips, he encouraged his fellow travelers with his prayers and cheered us with his humor and storytelling. Even while trekking under a scorching sun along difficult byways or climbing exhausting Andean trails, I never saw him discouraged. On the contrary, he motivated us with his enthusiasm. His extraordinary stamina was impressive. On wearisome all-day trips, even though he was generally the most senior in years of those accompanying him, he could manage the steep tracks, be among the first to arrive at nightfall, and be ready to preach in the evening service!

Don Pedro did not have any trouble accommodating himself to the inconveniences of rural communities. As in every other place, he was sincerely esteemed; people loved his caring, fatherly style and appreciated his keen interest in their well-being. Friends in Zulia saw that he liked to eat chontaduros (a small pitted fruit of the palm tree), and they always made sure he took some back to Bogotá! Understanding the deficiencies in their health, Don Pedro introduced rural farmers to some practical ideas for crop diversification in that area, encouraging them, for example, where it was appropriate to plant citrus fruits. Often their modest economy was depressed by the non-existence of roads and facilities to market their produce or to obtain necessities. He used the Bible to show them not only God's plan of salvation, but God's principles for honest

Don Pedro's voice was heard over the radio in a number of Spanish-speaking nations

and efficient improvement. As in other emerging evangelical Christian communities, his holistic approach brought an awakening of hope to Zulia. The solid preparation given by Don Pedro led to eight men from that congregation eventually becoming lay or fulltime pastors.[4]

Pedro Gutiérrez always dressed respectfully for ministerial functions, whether public or in the homes. He planned thoughtfully and conducted church services with reverence and dignity. It was both motivating and assuring to observe Don Pedro's life of perseverance and fidelity. During the year 1986, I had the joy of serving alongside him when he worked with the struggling La Clarita congregation in northwest Bogotá. He was never remiss in his commitments, even during inclement weather. Treachery on the streets at night and the chaotic public transport systems of that time never deterred him from traveling between the church and his home in the south of the city.

Don Pedro was seldom ill during his lifetime. He did have an appendectomy and on another occasion suffered the removal of his gallbladder. During one period when he pastored in Magangué, he became ill from overwork with the church's construction projects. Consequently, in counseling pastors he said: "Eat enough, but no more; and do not eat hurriedly.

Don Pedro was a reader and a scholar

Never take charge of building projects. As a result of making myself responsible for every detail of erecting the temple and school in Magangué, I suffered nervous tension and was not able to preach well." When he was almost 90 years old and suffering from diabetes in Miami, his doctor gave instructions that he measure his sugar count daily. Nevertheless, if friends asked about when he last took this count, this was his usual crisp reply: "I only do that on Saturdays." So they refrained from asking! But it is certainly true that Don Pedro enjoyed comparatively wonderful health throughout most of his life.

"The Righteous Shall Flourish Like a Palm Tree"

Pedro Gutiérrez was a practical man but also a scholar. He had the linguistic ability to benefit from his books in English. Among his library collection,[10] he particularly recommended "The Pilgrim's Progress"; "I love this book," he would say. Other titles he particularly enjoyed were "The Way of God," "The Spanish Brothers," and "All of Grace." In his sermons, he used illustrations from the Bible itself, sometimes from his books, but often from his own experiences.

His preaching was well structured. He once said, "I look for excellence. Nowadays, many Bible teachers go off in tangents and do not edify. I recommend expository preaching." Rarely did he finish preaching without inviting his hearers to come to Jesus Christ, and he was gentle and discerning with those who responded. When leading seekers to the Lord, he prayed for them with characteristic prudence and transparent sincerity. Hundreds were won to Christ through his preaching and counseling. He made it a priority to visit the sick and the needy and never failed to intercede for them in his own thoughtful way. From his home in Miami, when quite failed in his energies, he would talk and pray on the phone with the infirm and their relatives and lovingly counsel with those far and near who sought him out.

Through the ministry of Don Pedro and his wife, some particularly gifted people, like Víctor Garrido, were won to Christ. In 1958, Víctor, along with his wife Lura, wrote two hymns[11] that became very popular among Latin Christians, "I was Chosen by God" (Escogido fui de Dios),[14] and "I am the

Vine" (Yo soy la Vid). Don Pedro's spiritual and ministerial stature were everywhere genuinely acknowledged. The priority of prayer in his life was manifestly evident as was his good judgment. His advice and mediation were frequently sought after when conflicts arose between church members or when unresolved tensions existed among church or denominational leaders. They counted on his discreet discernment and his reconciling spirit. He was a quiet and peaceful man with a humble heart void of any resentment.

Despite being a man with notable accomplishments in planting churches, in vital leadership roles with the Latin America Mission, and later with the Inter-American Mission as well as serving on diverse committees, Don Pedro was never imperious or rigid. Nor did he pursue personal preferences. He was not bothered when his unique abilities in ministry and leadership were overlooked. On the contrary, he was consistently unassuming and self-effacing. Throughout his ministry, he was repeatedly obliged to put up with mediocre pastoral housing. During mission trips, he was often hosted in shack-like dwellings with very few amenities. In those situations, a "biological exigency" during the night demanded creative management! Then there was the "music" of roosters under the rough floorboards with their predawn calls to rural beginnings. But contingencies like these never disheartened Pastor Gutiérrez.

On another level Don Pedro made it his business to intercede for world leaders and sometimes even correspond with them. U.S. President Ronald Reagan and British Prime Minister Margaret Thatcher duly acknowledged his effort. Here is one such reply, dated July 13, 1987:

> Dear Mr. Gutiérrez, The Prime Minister asked me
> to thank you for your recent letter. Mrs. Thatcher

"THE MODEST GIANT FROM QUINDÍO"

is most grateful to you for your kind thought in writing.

Yours sincerely, – L. Gilchrist

Wherever Don Pedro and his wife lived, their home was a haven for needy individuals, some of whom were cared for indefinitely. In 1979, at the age of 65, he managed to build his own small house, the only one he ever possessed. This was not far from the Inter-American High School, where he and Teresa enjoyed cordial friendship with the staff and rector, Dr. George Medina. During the building of a spacious annex to accommodate the primary school section and an auditorium, Don Pedro took special interest in the construction workers themselves. Once a week, before work began in the early morning, he gathered them together, spoke to them, and prayed with them. On several occasions, I was a witness of the remarkable

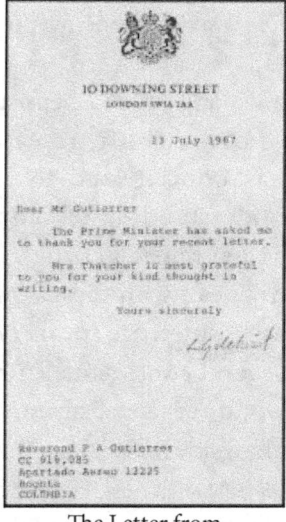

The Letter from Margaret Thatcher

Before their workday began, Don Pedro preached to them

reverence of these dear men, for they were clearly touched with the presence of God among them. In later years, with Don Pedro's help, two congregations were begun in that new facility.

Don Pedro's sons have been a special honor to their parents. Juan David, the younger of the two, is a gifted poet. The elder, Pedro Luis, became a professor of oncology and biochemistry whose scientific research has contributed to the understanding of cancer and of remedial drugs. He has dealt with these issues as a conference speaker on several continents. In his world of evangelism and pastoral ministries, Don Pedro served alongside men of like stature. Among these I mention: Dayton Roberts, Ernest Fowler, Harry Strachan, Robert Reed, David Howard, Burton Biddulph, Eugene Wittig, and Bruce Hess. He was also associated with the labors of Willie Easton, Lorenzo Emery, William Thompson, Benjamin Pearson, Bill Gillam, John Palmer, and John Harbinson – all foreigners because, at the time, Latin church leadership was still in its infancy. Indeed, leaders and church workers of different denominations in Colombia, Central America, and Miami genuinely respected Pedro Gutiérrez.

Don Pedro with his son, Dr. Peter L. Gutiérrez (Bogotá, 1985)

After moving to Miami in 1989 with Doña Teresa and their adopted son, Daniel, Don Pedro saw solid growth in the OMS church he served there. They came back to Colombia for a short time. Before returning to Miami in December 1991, OMS pastors and missionaries honored them with a special farewell event[12] to mark their gratitude to God for Don Pedro's 54 years in the Christian ministry.

Back in Miami, his congregation continued to grow. However,

with increasing age, Don Pedro became less steady on his feet and found it more difficult to get around. For this reason, he resorted more frequently to correspondence and the telephone. He still managed to preach, teach, and maintain contact with his network of friends in the U.S. and in Colombia. Some believers, before beginning their workday, would phone and ask him to pray with them. Without fail, he endeavored to encourage them with Bible comments, his caring words, and prayers.

It was in Miami on Sunday March 13, 2005, after teaching his morning Bible class in church, that at 3:30 p.m. Don Pedro suffered congestive heart failure. He died on the way to hospital. Thus, as simply as that, Pedro Gutiérrez Santamaría, this friend of so very many for so long, entered the presence of his Lord. He had arrived at his final abode. Who would not wish it to be thus at the end of life!

For more than seven decades, Don Pedro stood faithfully by his boyhood commitment to Christ. His was indeed a life of love and devotion to the Master. Has there ever been in Colombia another who served the Lord in this holy calling so triumphantly over such a span of years? Along with all who have had the privilege of knowing him, we praise the God of heaven for this modest but illustrious preacher of the Gospel and for the blessing to the church through his labors. The nation of Colombia has certainly been highly honored by this distinguished emissary of Christ, the Reverend Pedro Gutiérrez.

– Jim Smyth, Carlisle, Pennsylvania, USA
March 6, 2010

Counseling and praying with
friends near and far

Chapter 6

Tributes

Rev. Bruce Hess

MY FRIEND, DON PEDRO:
A TIRELESS WORKER, AN ENCOURAGER;
A MAN OF INTEGRITY AND OF SOUND
PRINCIPLES; A HUMBLE MAN; A SERVANT
OF GOD.

I came to know, and to work alongside Don Pedro during the 1970s and 1980s. I called him simply, Don Pedro, or Brother Pedro. He and his wife Fanny joined the national church of the Oriental Missionary Society[2] to serve in the work that the Mission had been doing for a long time in Colombia. They came to us with a vast understanding of Christian service in both Central America and northern Colombia.

As a pastor, preacher, and mentor, Don Pedro counseled, discipled, guided, and nurtured young pastors with great tact and wisdom from God. As vice president of the Association of Inter-American Evangelical Churches, his skillful leadership, combined with his tender spirit and humility, fostered spiritual and moral integrity in developing congregations. Young pastors always came to him with respect and confidence.

He was a real Barnabas; "Barnabas (which is translated Son of Encouragement) ... took (Saul) and brought him to the apostles." Saul, who later became Paul, saw in Barnabas a man of sterling character (Acts 4:36-37; 9:27).

I remember Don Pedro, too, as an administrator who inspired confidence by his courage. He could handle complicated issues with unusual insight. In committee, he never failed to vote with honest sincerity, never deviating from the truth. This was especially apparent when in 1980 the OMS-sponsored Inter-American High School in Bogotá faced a difficult situation with the Ministry of Education. His vote was crucial to save the school and make it possible for this Christian school to continue educating and serving the children of the city.

Don Pedro was like a father to everyone, not just because of his many years of experience, but because of his walk with the Lord. I cannot read the verses of I John 2:12-14 without thinking of Don Pedro; in part it says, "I have written to you, fathers, because you have known Him who is from the beginning." I thank God for this man of integrity and ethical principles.

The mature God-given judgment of this, His servant, will live forever in the memory and in the lives of many of us who knew him.

Yes, I knew Don Pedro. He was my trustworthy friend.

With much appreciation.

– Bruce R. Hess

Houghton, New York

Ubaldo Restan Padilla

Rev. Pedro Gutiérrez was one of the founders and president for ten years of the Association of Evangelical Churches of the Caribbean, an organization that today has more than 860 churches in Colombia and Venezuela. Between 1938 and 1990, he planted and contributed to the planting of more than 25 churches in Bogotá and in cities, towns, and villages of the Colombian costal region.

I welcome the publication of this book and especially encourage new generations of Christian leaders to read this biography. Among other things, it gives us some historical background to Christianity in Colombia, and it provides us with insights regarding the qualities and characteristics of a true apostle of Jesus Christ in the twenty-first century.

– Ubaldo Restan Padilla
Director of CIPEP,[13] Colombia

Rev. Gregorio Landero

I met the Rev. Pedro Gutiérrez when I was very young. At that time he was the pastor of the AIEC church in Montería, Colombia. What I remember most about him was his image as a pioneer of the evangelistic outreach in the south of Córdoba state. While a pastor in Montería, Don Pedro traveled around the towns, the country areas, and the regions beyond by horseback, by mule, or on foot, always sowing the seed of the divine Word. He was a man with a passion for preaching the sacred Gospel of Jesus Christ; this was at all times his primary interest. Don Pedro was highly respected and was recognized as an excellent expositor of the sacred Scriptures. He was an authority on doctrinal matters and a natural leader to whom we, the national church leadership, gave earnest heed. He motivated us because we knew he was taking care of us and of the new congregations. His favorite verse was Romans 1:17 – "The just shall live by faith."

– Rev. Gregorio Landero
Pioneer of evangelical social efforts in Colombia

Teresa Lizarazo Gutiérrez

March 13, 2005 was the last day that the Lord gave him on the earth. It was a Sunday, and, as was his practice, he taught his Sunday school class at the church where we attended, The Community of Jesus. I remember that, in this class of about 15 people, we always enjoyed Don Pedro's expositions. That makes me think about what he really was: a servant of the Lord who was faithful until death. We remember him also as a pastor who dedicated his entire life to the salvation of lost souls. He was always handing out tracts, sharing the message of the Lord with all who crossed his paths, and constantly concerned for the believers in his church.

As a husband, he was the best of the best; loving, kind, compassionate and respectful; that was Don Pedro. I thank God for being able to share 29 years of marriage alongside this servant of God. We miss him a lot, and I hold him in my heart as the great servant of God that he was.

– Teresa Gutiérrez

Daniel Javier Gutiérrez

I remember him as the best father in the world. Every day he warmed up my dinner. When he passed away, I asked my mom, "Who will warm up my dinner now?" I keep him in my heart as my own wonderful father. He was always watching out for me. I will forever miss him. I remember that he usually went for the mail; now I am doing that chore. And I will wait for my mom at our door, as he always used to do.

– Daniel Javier Gutiérrez

Endnotes

1. The Miami based *Latin America Mission* (LAM) was founded in 1921. The *Bible Seminary of Costa Rica* (*Latin America Bible Seminary*), the *Bible Institute* in Costa Rica, and the *Costa Rican Association of Bible Churches* referred to are organizations of the LAM. The *Association of Evangelical Churches of the Caribbean* (AIEC) was founded in Colombia by the Strachans in 1937 (See 3).

2. The *Association of Inter-American Evangelical Churches of Colombia* (ASODIEICO, initially identified as SMI) was founded in 1951. The denomination became known in 1998 as the *Inter-American Evangelical Church of Colombia* (IGLEICO). This and a sister denomination called the *Federation of Christian Fellowship Churches of Colombia* [*Iglesias Cristianas Confraternidad de Colombia*, begun in January 1988] and also the *Peniel Bible Institute* are fruit of the **One Mission Society** (OMS), originally known as the *Oriental Missionary Society*. Charles and Lettie Cowman (compiler of the renowned devotional book *Streams in the Desert*) founded OMS in Japan in 1901.

3. Harry and Susan Strachan: European missionaries who founded the *Latin America Mission*.

4. For English readers who may wish to know, the leaders and pastors to whom reference is made are: Obelio Sema (Pauna / San Martín), Eraclio Santamaría (Briceño), José Sema (Juan José Rondón, Bogotá), Marco Hernández (Cunday, Tolima), and Miguel Hernández (Moniquirá and Villa of the Alps, Bogotá). Later, another

associate, Alfredo Pulido, became the pastor in Guarumal (Zulia). Additionally, of the children who attended our Bible classes in the shade of some trees when the church in Zulia was in its infancy, one, Pedro Buitrago Casteblanco, became the pastor in Pauna, and another, Edwin Santamaría, a pastor in Maripí, Boyacá.

5. The *Christian & Missionary Alliance* denomination (C&MA) was founded by Dr. Albert Benjamin Simpson in 1887 and began outreach in Colombia in 1923 in the city of Ipiales (Nariño).

6. The *Inter-American High School* was founded in south Bogotá by OMS in 1964. It was actually a development of the OMS *Fourth Street Church* grade school in the city center. It began c.1950.

7. Founded in 1944 by OMS, the *Biblical Seminary of Colombia* (SBC), now known as the *University Foundation, Biblical Seminary of Colombia* (FUSBC), is an institution of higher education and was accredited in 2000 by the *Ministry of Education* in Colombia. In 1970, it opened an extension in Sincelejo under the AIEC.[1]

8. *Hammered as Gold* by David Howard (Harper and Row, 1969).

9. For English readers who may be interested: Next to Don Pedro in the photo is Adam Gómez, one of his disciples in Montería. In the center is Regina Romero. She and her husband Roberto Calderón pastored in Sincelejo for many years until the death of Roberto; beside her is the Canadian missionary, Alice Baker (LAM).[1]

10. Other books in his library that Don Pedro especially treasured were *The First Hundred Years of the Gospel in Colombia* by Francisco José Ordoñez (c.1966, in the C&MA Bible Institute library in Armenia); *El Encuentro* (2nd Edition, published by CLC); *The Evangelical Work in Colombia* (a history of the C&MA in Colombia during the early years) by Dr. Clyde Taylor; and *Lend Me the Tatabra*. (*Tatabra*: A Bible bound with leather from the *tatabra*, an animal that is also very edible).

11. See #340 and #402 in the *Celebremos Su Gloria* hymnbook (1992, *Libros Alianza*, TX and *Libros Cali*).

12. Among the participants at this event were the following clergy: Howard Biddulph, Carlos Cabrera, Bernabé Góngora, Anibal Alzate, and Randall Spacht.

13. The *Corporate Institute for Pastoral Education* (CIPEP), founded in 1981, is a ministry associated with the *Latin America Mission*.

14. Translation of the Spanish hymn, "*Escogido fui de Dios*":

> I was chosen by my God in the Beloved,
>   Blessed by Him in heav'nly places in Jesus Christ my Lord.
> This He purposed long before the world's creation, -
>   According to His will.
>
>   *[Refrain]*
>   *I am safe in Jesus' love; no one can harm me there;*
>   *Not the forces of this world or Satan and his host.*
>   *In this life I walk securely without fear or care,*
>   *Since my God has chosen me.*
>
> When I trusted in the word of God's salvation,
>   I received the seal of promise – the Holy Spirit giv'n
> As the guarantee of life with God in heaven, -
>   I was chosen by my God. *[Refrain]*
>
> He chose me for the praises of His glory,
>   And made me sit together with Christ in heav'nly realms,
> This He did to show His wondrous grace in Jesus, -
>   In the ages yet to come. *[Refrain]*
>
> Víctor Garrido
> Translated by Sara Leone, c. 1999

Young Men of the Cross is the story of One Mission Society's commitment to do something never before attempted—to place the Gospel message in every home in a nation. Their target was Japan, which at the time had 10.4 million homes. The Great Village Campaign was launched in 1913 with young Japanese evangelists carrying Scriptures to thousands of homes on small islands, in dense forests, and across barely accessible mountain ranges. In 1917, ten young men from God's Bible School in Cincinnati volunteered to work with the Japanese evangelists to complete this monumental task.

The Second Crusade, a sequel to *Young Men of the Cross*, tells of One Mission Society's post-World War II attempt to again reach every home in Japan with the gospel. This time, the program was called the Every Creature Crusade (ECC, now known as Every Community for Christ), and young college students joined national coworkers in spreading the gospel in Japan. Later, crusaders were sent to Korea, Taiwan, and Hong Kong to take the ECC program to those OMS fields as well. One OMS leader said of the effect of the ECC in his life: "As our crusade team moved from town to town and witnessed the salvation of hundreds and the planting of scores of churches, it was this more than anything else that drew many of us back to those fields as career missionaries."

My life story begins with a preacher who, by the leading of the Spirit, refused to end a service until my father, a successful businessman, had given his heart to the Lord. I eventually followed in my father's footsteps into full-time ministry, but only after overcoming self-doubt and self-consciousness in my ability to share the gospel.

God took that doubt away when a young man gave his heart to the Lord after I told him about Jesus. From that moment on, in Taiwan, the Philippines, and other places where I served, I saw the tremendous hand of the Lord at work as I allowed Him to lead and work through me. My desire is that you will be inspired and motivated to serve the Lord as freely and willingly as I was privileged to do for many years. May you, by God's grace, determine to live with no reserves, no retreats, and no regrets.

Valetta lost her young son Danny to leukemia; her husband Henry succumbed to Hodgkin's disease a few years later; then she lost her remaining two children in a tragic car accident. Her new reality was nearly unbearable, but when offered a secure position in her father's business, Valetta refused. The Lord had called her and Henry into ministry, and there was a mountain of unfinished business.

Today, Valetta has traveled the world, sharing Christ and teaching Christians how to share Christ in their communities. Thousands have been saved, and countless more inspired in their walk with the Lord. Valetta's story will touch you, move you, and challenge you to let God do as he desires in and through your life, enabling you to minister to others in ways you never would have imagined possible.

www.ingramcontent.com/pod-product-compliance
Lightning Source LLC
Chambersburg PA
CBHW070154080526
44586CB00015B/1983